A TALE OF TWO CITIES

Dickens's Revolutionary Novel

TWAYNE'S MASTERWORK STUDIES
Robert Lecker, General Editor

A TALE OF
TWO CITIES

Dickens's Revolutionary Novel

Ruth Glancy

TWAYNE PUBLISHERS • BOSTON
A Division of G. K. Hall & Co.

Twayne's Masterwork Studies No. 89

A Tale of Two Cities: Dickens's Revolutionary Novel
Ruth Glancy

Copyright 1991 by G. K. Hall & Co.
All rights reserved.
Published by Twayne Publishers
A division of G. K. Hall & Co.
70 Lincoln Street
Boston, Massachusetts 02111

Copyediting supervised by Barbara Sutton.
Book production by Janet Z. Reynolds.
Typeset by Compset, Inc., Beverly, Massachusetts.

10 9 8 7 6 5 4 3 2 1 (hc)
10 9 8 7 6 5 4 3 2 1 (pb)

Library of Congress Cataloging-in-Publication Data
Glancy, Ruth F., 1949–
    A tale of two cities : Dicken's revolutionary novel / Ruth Glancy.
        p.   cm.—(Twayne's masterwork studies ; no. 89)
    Includes bibliographical references (p.   ) and index.
    ISBN 0-8057-8088-2 (hc).—ISBN 0-8057-8552-3 (pb)
        1. Dickens, Charles, 1812–1870. Tale of two cities. 2. France—
History—Revolution, 1789–1799—Literature and the revolution.
I. Title. II. Series.
PR4571.G43   1991
823'.8—dc20   91-3251

contents

note on the references

For years the Oxford Illustrated Dickens has been the standard scholarly edition of Dickens's works, but more accessible and more useful editions are now available. I have used Oxford University Press's World's Classics edition of *A Tale of Two Cities* (1988) for all references. This edition contains an introduction and excellent, detailed annotations by Andrew Sanders, which are particularly necessary for understanding the many historical references in the novel. This edition also contains a chronology of the events of the French Revolution side by side with a chronology of the events in the novel. Where possible I have used World's Classics editions in referring to Dickens's works; otherwise, references are to Penguin editions or the Oxford Illustrated Dickens edition. Oxford University Press is working on the Clarendon Edition, which will provide definitive texts of all the novels; *A Tale of Two Cities* will soon be available in this edition.

It was difficult to obtain a good edition of Thomas Carlyle's *The French Revolution* until it appeared in a World's Classics edition in 1989, with annotations by Kenneth Fielding and David Sorensen. This difficult book is an important complement to *A Tale of Two Cities*, and although modern readers may not feel like carrying it about in their back pocket, as Dickens did when he was writing his novel, it is still well worth dipping into.

References to Shakespeare's *Hamlet* are given standard act, scene, and line numbers, so that any edition of the play may be used.

CHARLES DICKENS
Portrait by Herbert Watkins, 1859
Reproduced courtesy of the Dickens House, London

chronology:
charles dickens's life and works

1812	Charles John Huffam Dickens born 7 February at Landport, Portsea, second child of John and Elizabeth Dickens. Of six following brothers and sisters, four survive.
1814	John Dickens, a clerk in the navy pay office, moves the family to London.
1817	Family moves to Chatham, Kent.
1821	Charles attends William Giles's school, Chatham. An idyllic time for him, reading, writing plays, acting. Lives beside childhood love, Lucy Stroughill.
1822	Family moves back to a poor part of London.
1824	John Dickens imprisoned three months in the Marshalsea Prison for debt. Charles employed in Warren's Blacking Factory, pasting labels on bottles; is sent to live alone in lodgings. John released in May on receipt of a legacy. Charles enrolled at Wellington House Academy in the autumn. Is bitter for the rest of his life that his mother wished him to remain at Warren's.
1827	Charles leaves school, employed as solicitor's clerk.
1830	Studies independently at the British Museum library. Learns shorthand and becomes a freelance court stenographer. Falls in love with Maria Beadnell, but her family intervenes and puts an end to the liaison.
1831	Enters the House of Commons Gallery as a reporter for the *Mirror of Parliament*.
1832	Considers an acting career, but misses the audition owing to a bad cold. Is parliamentary reporter for the *True Sun*. The first Reform Bill passes.
1833	First sketch, "A Dinner at Poplar Walk," published in December issue of *Monthly Magazine*.

1834	Joins staff of the *Morning Chronicle*. Several more sketches published this year.
1836	*Sketches by Boz* published. *Pickwick Papers* begins as a monthly serial, published by Chapman and Hall. On 2 April marries Catherine Hogarth, daughter of George Hogarth, editor of the *Evening Chronicle*. Second series of *Sketches by Boz* published. Leaves the House of Commons Gallery.
1837	Victoria becomes queen. Charles, Jr., first of 10 children, born. *Pickwick Papers* concludes. Dickens's sister-in-law Mary Hogarth dies unexpectedly in his house, a blow from which he never fully recovers. Becomes editor of *Bentley's Miscellany* and begins *Oliver Twist* for monthly publication in that journal.
1838	Begins *Nicholas Nickleby* in monthly parts for Chapman and Hall. Mary ("Mamie") born in March.
1839	*Oliver Twist* concludes in April; Dickens resigns from *Bentley's*. *Nicholas Nickleby* concludes in October. Second daughter, Kate, born.
1840	For Chapman and Hall begins a weekly journal, *Master Humphrey's Clock*, in which *The Old Curiosity Shop* is serialized.
1841	*Barnaby Rudge* runs in *Master Humphrey's Clock*. Son Walter born.
1842	Tours North America, January to June. Visits Philadelphia prison. *American Notes* published in October.
1843	*Martin Chuzzlewit* begins in monthly installments. *A Christmas Carol* published in December.
1844	Quarrel with Chapman and Hall. *Martin Chuzzlewit* concludes. Dickens moves to Italy. Christmas book, *The Chimes*, published in December. Dickens returns to London briefly to read it to friends. Fifth child, Francis, born.
1845	Returns to England in July. Edits the *Daily News* for a few weeks. Sixth child, Alfred, born. Christmas book, *The Cricket on the Hearth*, published in December. Dickens is involved in amateur theatricals.
1846	*Pictures from Italy* published by Bradbury and Evans. Dickens moves to Switzerland in May. Begins *Dombey and Son* in monthly installments for Bradbury and Evans. Christmas book, *The Battle of Life*, is published.
1847	Lives in Lausanne, then Paris. Visits the sites of the French Revolution. No Christmas book. Seventh child, Sydney, born.

Chronology

Helps Angela Burdett Coutts, a wealthy philanthropist, establish Urania Cottage, a home for homeless women. Works closely with the home for the next 10 years.

1848   *Dombey and Son* completed in April. *The Haunted Man* published for Christmas. Outbreak of revolutions all over Europe.

1849   *David Copperfield* begins in monthly installments. Eighth child, Henry, born. Dickens writes *The Life of Our Lord* for his children (unpublished until 1934).

1850   Establishes a new weekly journal, *Household Words*. Visits Paris. *David Copperfield* concludes. Third daughter, Dora, born.

1851   Visits Paris. *A Child's History of England* published in *Household Words*. Dora dies.

1852   *Bleak House* begins in monthly installments. Tenth child, Edward ("Plorn"), born.

1853   Tours Italy and Switzerland. *Bleak House* concludes. First charity reading of *A Christmas Carol*.

1854   *Hard Times* serialized in *Household Words*.

1855   *Little Dorrit* begins in monthly installments. Dickens visits Paris.

1856   Buys Gad's Hill Place, Kent. Collaborates on *The Wreck of the Golden Mary* for *Household Words*'s Christmas number.

1857   Acts in Wilkie Collins's play *The Frozen Deep* and meets the young actress Ellen Ternan, soon to become his companion. *Little Dorrit* concludes. Dickens's walking tour of the Lake District with Wilkie Collins results in *The Lazy Tour of Two Idle Apprentices* for *Household Words*. Collaborates on *The Perils of Certain English Prisoners* for *Household Words*'s Christmas number.

1858   First series of public readings. Separates from Catherine.

1859   Quarrels with Bradbury and Evans and returns to Chapman and Hall. Establishes a new journal, *All the Year Round*, in which *A Tale of Two Cities* is serialized. Darwin's *Origin of Species* and Karl Marx's *Critique of Political Economy* published.

1860   *The Uncommercial Traveller* serialized in *All the Year Round*, followed by *Great Expectations*.

1861   *Great Expectations* concludes in August. Holds second series of public readings.

1864	Begins *Our Mutual Friend* in monthly installments.
1865	*Our Mutual Friend* concludes. On 9 June Dickens is involved in the Staplehurst train derailment while returning from Paris with Ellen Ternan. Unhurt himself, Dickens tends the wounded and dying.
1866	Holds third series of public readings.
1867	Goes on reading tour of America.
1868	Farewell reading tour begins.
1869	Reading tour curtailed due to failing health.
1870	Begins *The Mystery of Edwin Drood* in April. On 9 June dies at Gad's Hill. Buried in Westminster Abbey 14 June.

Literary and
Historical Context

1

Dickens's Times

"It was the best of times, it was the worst of times, it was the age of wisdom, it was the age of foolishness, it was the epoch of belief, it was the epoch of incredulity, it was the season of Light, it was the season of Darkness, it was the spring of hope, it was the winter of despair."[1] In his famous opening lines for *A Tale of Two Cities,* Dickens was sounding the keynote not just for the time of the first French Revolution, the setting of his novel, but also for the age in which he lived. Writing in 1859, exactly 70 years after the storming of the Bastille, Dickens shared his contemporaries' ambivalence about the revolutionary period: while they celebrated the overthrow of the corrupt feudal system of prerevolutionary France, they abhorred the violent means by which that overthrow was brought about and feared that such a revolution might erupt again, but this time in England.

This ambivalence was felt, not just by Victorians like Dickens, but by those who lived through the Revolution and commented on it in the early years of the nineteenth century. The French Revolution coincided with a radical change in the way writers of the time viewed themselves and society, a change generally referred to now as the romantic movement. From the eighteenth-century emphasis on man as a social being, on a belief in the importance of reason and man's ability to discover all truths through the exercise of his intellect, came a reaction against such beliefs. The new generation of writers and thinkers led by the poets Wordsworth and Coleridge, Shelley and Keats, placed a new emphasis on man as an individual, on the value of the common man, and on the power of the creative imagination. These new ideas were fed by the events of the French Revolution, and at first the revolution was viewed with enthusiasm: here was the ordinary citizen rising up against oppression, throwing off the outdated traditions and worthless pomp and ceremony that had surrounded the old aristocracies. The heroes of the Revolution who came up from the ranks of the ordinary people were hailed as the messiahs of a new order. The romantic writers in Britain talked about "the spirit of the age," how the French Revolution seemed "the rising orb of liberty."[2] At once political commentators such as Thomas Paine saw the benefits of such a revolution occurring in Britain. But as the months passed and the revolutionaries became increasingly violent, culminating in the execution of the French royal family and the infamous Reign of Terror, which saw more than 2,800 people guillotined in Paris alone in just two years, observers in England became increasingly sickened and frightened by what they saw. Hazlitt's "rising orb" became "quenched in darkness and in blood." The season of Light had become the season of Darkness; the spring of hope had become the winter of despair.

The fear that such a revolution could occur in Britain was largely an unspoken one, for Britain had always been proud of its nonviolent history of moderate reform; the "Glorious" or "Bloodless Revolution" of 1688 had been so called because of its lack of bloodshed when the Catholic King James II had been replaced by the Protestant monarchs William and Mary. Insisting on his divine right to rule, James had set aside laws and overridden Parliament so as to oppress the Protestant majority. With the crowning of his Protestant daughter Mary and her Dutch husband William a more tolerant age emerged in which the power of the monarchy was curtailed and the supremacy of Parliament was reaffirmed. In 1689 the Bill of Rights established these changes, as well as guaranteeing certain rights to individuals. So far-reaching were the results of this "revolution" that the governing of the country continued relatively unchanged until Dickens's time.

Queen Victoria's England was a very different country from the England of William and Mary, however. The Industrial Revolution had by now transformed the landscape and the way of life of most of the people, resulting in the contradictions chosen by Dickens for his opening. The invention of machinery for manufacturing previously done by hand and the modernization of farming methods in smaller private farms meant a rapid movement of the population into the towns, particularly in the north of England. Overcrowding, disease, hunger, long hours of work, and mindless, repetitive labor characterized the new life for this new class of urban poor.

While the causes of their suffering were rather different from those that led to the French Revolution, the problems of the poor were very similar. In both cases the struggle was a class one; England was now a country of "Two Nations" as Disraeli put it, the rich and the poor, the governing and the governed. And for the working classes, as for the French peasantry, there seemed to be no way of improving their plight because they had no political voice. They had no vote and were not allowed to unionize. Many members of the upper classes feared even educating the poor, in case they would then become politically aware and eager to better themselves when it suited many people to have them as cheap labor. Most of their protests were orderly and peaceful marches, meetings, or strikes. But when violence did break out in the destruction of machinery, rick burning, or riots, people feared that a revolution as horrifying as the French one could after all happen in England. A few political thinkers believed that such a revolution was actually the answer to Britain's problems, but most people, like Dickens, feared the actions of the mob, having seen the bloody outcome of the 1789 revolution.

In 1855 Dickens wrote to a friend that he was frustrated at the alienation of ordinary people from public affairs, the result of years of being prevented from taking any part in parliamentary reform. He was worried that their apparent lack of interest was actually disguising a growing dissatisfaction: "And I believe the discontent to be so much the worse for smouldering, instead of blazing openly, that it is extremely like the general mind of France before the breaking out of the first Revolution, and is in danger of being turned by any one of a thousand accidents—a bad harvest—the last strain too much of aristocratic insolence or incapacity—a defeat abroad—a mere chance at home—into such a devil of a conflagration as never has been beheld since."[3] Dickens went on to suggest that, like the French aristocracy, the English gentility of 1855 were ignoring the signs: "So, every day, the disgusted millions with this unnatural gloom and calm upon them are confirmed and hardened in the very worst of moods. Finally, round all this is an atmosphere of poverty, hunger, and ignorant desperation, of the mere existence of which, perhaps not one man in a thousand . . . has the least idea." He wished the people would "array themselves peacefully" against the system, but feared their lethargy was an "awful symptom of the advanced state of their disease."

By 1859, when Dickens wrote *A Tale of Two Cities*, Britain had recovered from the Napoleonic Wars and was fast becoming the most powerful country in the world owing to its highly advanced technology and industrialization. London was now the center of world trade, culture, and ideas, taking over from the Paris of the previous century. But as Dickens's opening lines suggest, this "best of times" was still far from rosy for the majority of the population, who continued to suffer in overcrowded slums and squalid factories. The popular political theory of laissez-faire, which dictated that governments should not intervene in business, gave free rein to factory and mill owners to be as exploitive as they pleased. Unrest continued, surfacing in groups like the Chartists, working men who drew up a People's Charter advocating various election reforms. Despite a petition signed by over one million people, the movement failed to achieve its aim in the 1830s; in 1848 it failed again, despite huge popular support. The Chartists had to wait until the Reform Bill of 1867 to receive some of their demands. There was no bloody revolution, but Dickens and others deplored the snail's pace that the government took to achieve peaceful reform through the parliamentary process.

If the time of the Revolution in France was "the epoch of belief . . . the epoch of incredulity," so too were the 1850s in Britain. As the powerful church was one of the targets of the revolutionaries, Christian practice and belief were actually banned for a time during the Revolution, and the republicans perverted Christian symbols to their own ends. Philosophical thinking in mid-Victorian Britain was less radical, but there was a school of belief, led by the Utilitarians, that considered religion an outdated superstition, unnecessary to the reasonable man. The year 1859 saw the publication not just of *A Tale of Two Cities* but of Charles Darwin's *On the Origin of Species* as well. Incredulity had new weapons; belief was under attack, and Dickens was ready to defend it.

2

The Importance of the Work

A Tale of Two Cities has a unique place in the Dickens canon. Dickens wrote it in 1859, when he was at the height of his powers as a novelist. It was preceded by *Little Dorrit* and followed by *Great Expectations,* both novels of remarkable maturity and complexity. Although it has much in common with all of the novels of Dickens's maturity, it was regarded by Dickens himself as something of an experiment and has always been seen as untypical of a "Dickensian" novel. For some readers this is a drawback; for others it is an advantage. But how untypical is it really?

A Tale of Two Cities is unlike Dickens's other novels because of its historical setting. Although all the novels are rooted firmly in nineteenth-century England and address current issues and attitudes, only *A Tale of Two Cities* and his 1841 novel *Barnaby Rudge* revolve around a specific historical incident. Both novels describe dramatically the actions of a mob, but the tide of human emotion and violence whipped up in the Paris of 1789 in *A Tale of Two Cities* is given a much more substantial motivation than the often arbitrary and mindless brutality of the antipopery rioters of *Barnaby Rudge.* And here we can see how a *A Tale of Two Cities* is actually very typical of Dickens in its championing of the poor, and its attack on what to many Victorians were the "good old days," but which to Dickens were evil times fraught with injustice and oppression.

Dickens's approach to his subject is different in *A Tale of Two Cities* from the other novels, because now his focus, rather than being on character, is on the highly charged setting in which the action takes place. For many readers this is an insuperable drawback, depriving the novel of the wealth of often comic and always memorable characters—Sairey Gamp, Uriah Heep, Sam Weller—who people the Dickens world and give it its vitality. The characters in *A Tale of Two Cities* are much less memorable, with the exception of its hero, Sydney Carton, and its villain, Madame Defarge. Charles Darnay's family name, Evrémonde, suggests Everyman, or "all the world," and he serves this allegorical purpose rather than being memorably drawn. The minor characters, usually so vividly described, are representatives of a class rather than individuals. Three of the revolutionaries are identified only as Jacques One, Two, and Three, and Madame Defarge's merciless companion has no other name than The Vengeance. Dickens's purpose here was to show the dehumanizing effect of mass action, even though the motive behind the action may be human suffering. Against this mechanical, institutionalized force he sets the private heroism of his main characters, who suffer and die but remain totally human in the best sense.

In this *A Tale of Two Cities* is very much a Dickensian novel. At the heart of Dickens's life and work was his consciousness that love and compassion, the most important of all human attributes, are nurtured by imagination and a childlike perceptiveness and spontaneity. He railed against fashionable social philosophies like Utilitarianism that would turn people into numbers and sink the individual in the "common good." He railed against social inequalities that turned eager, loving children into hardened criminals through lack of education and lack of food. And he railed against any social system that set one class against another instead, as Scrooge's nephew says, of letting them think of people "as if they really were fellow-passengers to the grave, and not another race of creatures bound on other journeys."[1] All of these attitudes he saw played out in the French Revolution, from the aristocrat who starved his workers and could run over a poor child with less concern than if it had been his horse, to the republicans themselves, who at the height of the Terror equally could lose sight of the individual victims of their revenge.

A Tale of Two Cities may lack the breadth of character and humor of the more typically Dickensian novels, but its neatly interlocking plot, every incident and character essential to the working out of the design, is Dickens the storyteller at his best. Stylistically, too, A Tale of Two Cities demonstrates Dickens in full command of his text. His characteristic humor is less in evidence, but it is replaced by a powerful evocation of people swept up in an emotional and physical tide. The rhetoric of the novel is compelling and even frightening as it re-creates the sounds and rhythms of revolutionary Paris. And as the sounds begin to reverberate in a quiet Soho square, Dickens's mastery of the domestic scene is as finely felt as in any of his other novels.

Readers must come to A Tale of Two Cities with the sense of it as a complete work in itself, as Dickens intended when he urged his friends to read it all of a piece instead of in the weekly installments in which it was first published. Even without the comic vision that we associate with Dickens, taken in its entirety it does more than give us diluted Dickens, or Dickens on an off day, as some critics would have us believe. It has proven itself to be a classic of enduring dramatic power, revealing Dickens at his most descriptive and his most human.

3

Critical Reception

In a review of *Great Expectations*, the novel that succeeded *A Tale of Two Cities*, the *Eclectic Review* noted that Dickens's last two novels had been "rather severely handled by the critics. 'A Tale of Two Cities' pleased nobody."[1] This was not strictly true; a short review in the *Athenaeum* noted that "a hundred thousand readers have followed the exciting adventures of Doctor Manette and his charming daughter. The tale is told, and the audience of a hundred thousand, as the curtain drops, cry—Well done!"[2] The *Athenaeum* reviewer was happy to "echo the public voice" and admire the novel, but most of the critics writing in the intellectual and literary journals of the day considered popular success a good reason to condemn a work. If the public liked it, they certainly could not be seen to approve of it at all.

This attitude to Dickens's popularity was evident in a scathing attack by Sir James Fitzjames Stephen in the *Saturday Review*. After condemning the plot—"it would perhaps be hard to imagine a clumsier or more disjointed framework for the display of the tawdry wares which form Mr. Dickens's stock-in-trade"[3]—Stephen dismissed *A Tale of Two Cities* as a purely mechanical effort, producing grotesqueness and pathos through formula writing and trickery. He objected particularly to the "grotesqueness" of the speech of the French characters, whose French-sounding English he considered "misbegotten jargon" that "shows a great want of sensibility to the real requirements of art" (Stephen, 43). Finally, Stephen took Dickens to task for his history, criticizing his attack on the old aristocracy of France as grossly unfair. He objected also to Dickens's suggestion that the England of the present day was much superior to the England of the eighteenth century: "The childish delight with which Mr. Dickens acts Jack Horner, and says What a good boy am I, in comparison with my benighted ancestors, is thoroughly contemptible" (Stephen, 45).

"Christopher Grim" in the *Dublin University Magazine* shared Stephen's harsh condemnation, agreeing that Dickens's "*effects* are produced by some ridiculous trick or association attached to his characters." He too complained that the plot is "so clumsily put together that it is almost impossible to follow it" and that in his description of eighteenth-century England Dickens "indulges to excess in caricature."[4]

The reviewer for the *Critic* also criticized Dickens for comparing eighteenth-century England unfavorably with their present time; don't bad roads and bad kings exist in all ages, he argued. This critic did acknowledge that the novel yielded real delight, however, and was superior to most contemporary novels; only in comparison with Dickens's other works could it be called a failure.[5]

The *Eclectic* reviewer told an often-repeated story that Stephen's attack sent Dickens to bed for months, "in a state of [such] hopeless lethargy, that it needed the constant application of warm flannels and bathings of mustard and turpentine, and the united influence of at least a dozen physicians, to restore him to consciousness" (*Eclectic*, 459). Although Dickens was frequently upset by reviews he would actually have been much more concerned to know Thomas Carlyle's reaction, which fortunately was quite different: Carlyle considered the novel "wonderful!"[6] So did Dickens's friend John Forster, who in reviewing the novel anonymously for the *Examiner* concentrated on "its exquisite construction."[7] After Dickens's death Forster was a little less enthusiastic, considering the emphasis on plot rather than character not "an entirely successful experiment."[8]

A Tale of Two Cities continued to be a very popular work with the public, especially after its huge success as a stage play, *The Only Way,* which opened in London in 1899 and ran in Britain and the United States for years afterwards. Sir John Martin-Harvey's portrayal of Sydney Carton in this version transferred the interest of the play from the French Revolution to Carton's sacrifice, and dramatic and film versions since then have helped to make the book Carton's story. At the same time the passing of the years has distanced the novel's readers from the French Revolution; in 1859 it was still a fairly recent event, the significance of which was being discussed and written about daily, so Dickens's portrayal of it was of particular interest. Nowadays, the solitary, outcast hero is more likely to arouse the interest of the reader.

We know that Dickens himself considered the novel a bit of an experiment when he deliberately set out to write "*a picturesque story, rising in every chapter, with characters true to nature, but whom the story should express more than they should express themselves by dialogue*" (Forster, 2:281). Many critics since 1859 have considered the novel to be so much an experiment (and a failed one at that) as to be actually outside the Dickens canon. It tends to be the most popular Dickens novel with people who do not generally like Dickens, whereas loyal Dickensians usually cite *A Tale of Two Cities* as their least favorite. In many critical books on Dickens *A Tale of Two Cities* is either omitted or quickly dismissed for the "un-Dickensian" attributes brought about by Dickens's emphasis on the story: its lack of humor, its lack of comic and unforgettable characters, and its often melodramatic dialogue. Some early critics even thought it sounded as though it had been written by someone else and would have been better if it had. Margaret Oliphant, in a long overview of Dickens written a year after his death, thought that *A Tale of Two Cities* "might have been written by any new author, so little of Dickens there is in it. In short, we believe there are at least half-a-dozen writers extant who could have produced a piece a great deal more like the master, and with much more credible marks of authenticity."[9] George Gissing, whose *Charles Dickens: A Critical Study* was one of the first full-length books on Dickens, admitted that *A Tale of Two Cities* was "something like a true tragedy," but added that "many another man could have handled the theme as well, if not better."[10]

Other well-known critics writing around the turn of the twentieth century found *A Tale of Two Cities* wanting for a variety of reasons. Sir George Saintsbury considered the historical elements unreal, the Terror a "No Man's Land of time and space"[11] that was Dickens's world rather than the world of a historical period. A. W. Ward was willing to call the novel "an extraordinary *tour de force*,"[12] but he found the plot too contrived, although cleverly constructed.

There were admirers too. Edgar Shannon, writing in 1913, was willing to call *A Tale of Two Cities* Dickens's last great novel, arguing that at last Dickens had developed out of the melodramatic into the genuinely dramatic.[13] Edwin Percy Whipple had high praise for the "enthralling interest of the story,"[14] which he felt made *A Tale of Two Cities* one of the most exciting narratives in the whole of fiction. Whipple was one of many to praise Sydney Carton (probably the most misspelled of all literary names, by the way—he is "Sidney" in much of the criticism of the novel), finding his death scene "pathetic and noble . . . beyond almost any other in Dickens's work" (Whipple, 189). Whipple agreed with Richard Grant White that "Carton stands out as one of the noblest characters in the whole literature of fiction" (Whipple, 189). Ward too had found that Carton's self-sacrifice produced "a legitimate tragic effect" (Ward, 156). Only George Gissing felt that the novel left no strong impression on the mind, and even the figure of Carton "grows dim" (Gissing, 61).

For several years there was little written about the novel except for introductions to the many editions published throughout this century. It continued to be regarded as somehow not "Dickensian" and was therefore judged not for what it was, but for what it was not. Like the comic actor who has trouble being accepted in serious roles, Dickens has frequently been condemned for striking out in a new vein that was actually as "Dickensian" as the comic eccentrics and broad humor of his other novels, provided the reader comes to it without preconceived ideas about what he expects from a Dickens novel. Arthur Waugh, the editor of Chapman and Hall's famous Biographical edition of Dickens (1903), noted that *A Tale of Two Cities* differed from the other novels because it was conceived during the performance of a play, but gave it due credit for being an experiment. Whereas many critics have seen the novel as a failed attempt at tragedy that Dickens never repeated, Waugh saw it as "a story of new departures" that ushered in a new form of writing for Dickens. He noted that after *A Tale of Two Cities* the "old form of leisurely narrative was never to be returned to"[15] and that the later novels benefited from Dickens's concern in *A Tale of Two Cities* with incident and plot. Bernard Darwin attributed the well-knit plot to writer and friend Wilkie Collins's influence, but he found the novel "not quite the genuine Dickens." Like many readers, Darwin regretted the lack of Dickensian characters, but acknowledged that "by way of compensation Dickens was here at his very best as a descriptive writer."[16]

G. K. Chesterton and George Orwell, both well-known admirers of Dickens, took him to task for his portrayal of the French Revolution. Although Chesterton wrote of *A Tale of Two Cities* that "in dignity and eloquence it almost stands alone among his books," he disliked Carlyle's influence on it, finding both writers mistaken in seeing the Revolution "as a mere elemental outbreak of hunger or vengeance; they do not see enough that it was a war for intellectual principles."[17] Orwell accused Dickens of exaggerating the horrors of the Terror and found it ironic that although he was in sympathy with the ideals of the Revolution, he played a large part in making later generations think of the Revolution as a blood bath: "Thanks to Dickens, the very word 'tumbril' has a murderous sound; one forgets that a tumbril is only a sort of farm-cart."[18]

The latter half of this century has seen a positive deluge in articles and books about Dickens, and although *A Tale of Two Cities* is still not in the small group that take turns being regarded as the "best novel," it has now a much firmer claim to interest and relevance than was accorded it by its first critics. It is still sometimes decried for its popularity, much as Stephen condemned it in 1859; in reviewing public opinions of the novel, George Ford writes that *A Tale of Two Cities* is the only Dickens novel that appeals to the needs of the scullery maid, who "longs, not to enter the lives of others, but to behold herself in changed situations."[19] Angus Wilson declares it Dickens's "great middlebrow success."[20] The German critic Heinz Reinhold suggested that Stephen's vitriol was mostly political: a Conservative, Stephen resented the attack on the aristocracy in the novel, but hid his political objections behind criticism of the artistry of the book.[21] Wilson fears that he too may be accused of "artistic snobbery," but still cannot count it an artistic success. He does agree with Waugh, though, that the "paring down" of Dickens's writing in *A Tale of Two Cities* contributed to the tight construction of *Great Expectations*.

Biographers of Dickens have found much of interest in *A Tale of Two Cities*. They have pounced upon the name Charles Darnay and its closeness to Charles Dickens, and of course Dickens identifies himself with Sydney Carton in his preface to the novel, through his acting the part of Carton's literary predecessor Richard Wardour in the play *The Frozen Deep*, written by Wilkie Collins but heavily influenced and amended by Dickens. Because the novel was written around the time of Dickens's separation from his wife and new relationship with a young woman, Ellen Ternan, biographical critics have been quick to see Dickens's revolutionary subject as the projection of the revolution in his personal life. After being buried alive, like Manette, Dickens has to split himself into the two heroes Carton and Darnay so that one can be the scapegoat while the other wins the girl. In his 1988 biography, Fred Kaplan describes the Darnay/Carton double as "an antiphonal self-portrait that, while it emphasizes the heavy hand of the past and the potential for self-destruction, unites opposites into an idealized version of love."[22]

The many post-Freudian psychological interpretations have also concentrated on the significance of the double as well as on the complex family relationships raised by the novel's private and public stories. Lawrence Frank examines fathers and sons: Doctor Manette, in the role of son, witnesses a father's brutal rape, a "primal scene"; Darnay's career "reveals the son's complex, perhaps doomed, struggle to free himself from his father's tyranny."[23] Albert Hutter also examines generations in the novel, seeing the Evrémondes' rape as a primal scene that is parodied in Jerry Cruncher's relationship with his wife. Hutter attributes the novel's lack of critical popularity to Dickens's "historical oversimplification. . . . Carton's solution is that of any son—or class—that willingly accepts the pain or injustice inflicted upon it by parents or rulers, and such a solution is not particularly satisfying to most readers."[24]

A Tale of Two Cities has achieved new status and new serious study as a historical novel with the recent interest in that genre. It has always been admired by Marxist critics such as T. A. Jackson, who sees Carton's sacrifice, not as a solution, but as a "triumphantly redeeming escape" from a life of failure. In *A Tale of Two Cities* Dickens "gets nearer than ever to a positive assertion of revolution as the only road to hope, to justice, to peace and to general happiness."[25] A more balanced reading has been provided in several recent studies of the historical novel, but again there is disagreement over what point Dickens is making about the Revolution and how successful the novel is as historical fiction. In his influential study of the historical novel, Georg Lukács dismisses the Christian ethics of *A Tale of Two Cities* as "petty bourgeois humanism and idealism,"[26] but Dickens is defended by many later historians. Morton Zabel considers it the most powerful example of the nineteenth-century historical novel, and Dickens "the most eloquent voice of personal dissent and revolutionary challenge the English novel of his age can show."[27] Avrom Fleishman considers the lack of impressive characters a virtue rather than a flaw, finding the novel "one of the first historical novels to characterize and dramatize social groups as major carriers of the action."[28] Andrew Sanders warns against criticizing the novel for its lack of political solutions, arguing that Dickens was concerned with showing the causes of the Revolution and its effect. Carton's resurrection is "to be taken with full Christian force" as a "pattern for the redemption of society."[29]

A Tale of Two Cities has been consistently criticized for its flat characters, its lack of humor, and its staginess. The French critic Sylvère Monod is particularly comic about this aspect of the novel, pointing out the difficulties of Doctor Manette's wringing his hair, and the artist's even greater difficulties in illustrating the scene: "It demands a great deal of room, especially if you do it properly, with both hands, elbows raised symmetrically; so Manette has to be planted, legs apart, on one side of the picture; legs apart, because you can't wring your hair adequately with your hat on; and in a crowded etching, the only place for the hat is on the floor, between your feet."[30] Monod revised his formerly harsh opinion of *A Tale of Two Cities* in this article, finding in it, despite its faults, "the remarkable performance of a consummate artist" (Monod, 30). Monod has particular praise for Dickens's style, and indeed most critics have disagreed with John Gross's description of the style as "grey and unadorned."[31]

The many modern studies of the novel's historical importance, complex use of doubling, psychological truth, and stylistic and narrative sophistication testify to its enduring interest among literary critics as one of Dickens's great novels. Its continuing presence on school reading lists and in films and plays (an Anglo-French television version appeared in 1989) attests to its lasting popularity, not just with scullery maids, but with the many readers who find in *A Tale of Two Cities* the full range of Dickens's dramatic and narrative power.

4

"One of These Days": The Genesis of A Tale of Two Cities

The germ of *A Tale of Two Cities* had occurred to Dickens 14 years before he actually began the novel, while he was working on another story about self-sacrifice, a Christmas book called *The Battle of Life*. Writing to his friend and biographer John Forster in July 1846, Dickens says, "I have been thinking this last day or two that good Christmas characters might be grown out of the idea of a man imprisoned for ten or fifteen years: his imprisonment being the gap between the people and circumstances of the first part and the altered people and circumstances of the second, and his own changed mind" (Forster, 1:419)

Nine years later the idea of a story in two parts occurred to him again, and he noted it down in the Memoranda Book that he began compiling in 1855: "How as to a story in two periods—with a lapse of time between, like a French Drama?" At the same time he thought of several titles for such a story, one of which was "Memory Carton."[1] When these ideas finally came together as *A Tale of Two Cities* in 1859, the novel was in some ways a rewriting of the Christmas book, and a greatly improved one. Nowadays few people have even heard of *The Battle of Life*, whereas most of the English-speaking world can quote either the opening line of *A Tale of Two Cities* or Carton's memorable closing one. The Christmas book is also a "story in two periods," and the sacrifice is made by one sister for another, because they both love the same man. Pretending to elope with someone else, Marion goes away for six years, leaving the field clear for Alfred to transfer his affections to her elder sister, Grace. Dickens was disappointed in the book when he had finished it and told a friend that he might rework the theme again, "one of these days perhaps."[2] Curiously, "One of These Days" was one of several titles Dickens contemplated before he decided on *A Tale of Two Cities*.

Between 1845 and 1859, the quiet heroism of sisterly love in *The Battle of Life* became transformed into the more stirring and active heroism that was to become Sydney Carton. It was an exciting time for Victorians: explorations into uncharted and hostile reaches of the world were under way, and Dickens was following avidly the exploits of one expedition in particular, that of Sir John Franklin and his crew in their search for the Northwest Passage. When the expedition was lost, a search party brought back reports from Eskimos that the expedition members had resorted to cannibalism before their deaths. Dickens was outraged by the charge and defended them hotly in several articles in his weekly journal *Household Words*.

As well as wanting to defend Franklin from the charge of cannibalism, Dickens was also particularly fascinated by another aspect of the voyage, which emerged from current accounts: the friendship between Sir John Franklin and his coexplorer Sir John Richardson, a Scottish doctor and naturalist. Dickens wrote of this friendship to John Forster in 1856: "Lady Franklin sent me the whole of that Richardson memoir; and I think Richardson's manly friendship, and love of Franklin, one of the noblest things I ever knew in my life. It makes one's heart beat high, with a sort of sacred joy" (Forster, 2:399).

The search for such a friendship in his own life dominated Dickens's thoughts in the 1850s, a time of tremendous emotional upheaval for him. In 1836 he had married Catherine Hogarth, the daughter of a Scottish publisher. A marriage originally of affection rather than passion, it deteriorated rapidly into one of boredom for Dickens and by the 1850s had become an intolerable misery to him. Catherine remains a shadowy figure, but according to most sources it seems unlikely that she deserved Dickens's harsh criticism of her as a mother whose daughters "harden into stone figures of girls when they can be got to go near her, and have their hearts shut up in her presence as if they were closed by some horrid spring."[3] (Dickens uses this turning to stone metaphor frequently in *A Tale of Two Cities.*) Their incompatibility was one of temperament, intelligence, and general sensitivity, the "unsuitability of mind and purpose" that David Copperfield complains of in his marriage to Dora. For a man of such emotional vigor as Dickens, marriage to the wrong woman was an intolerable burden, which sent him in desperate search of relief from other sources until he finally left her in 1858.

Dickens's main source of solace in the years preceding the breakup of the marriage and the writing of *A Tale of Two Cities* was his friendship with another writer, Wilkie Collins, with whom he collaborated on stories of heroic friendship. In 1856 they wrote together a Christmas number for *Household Words*, *The Wreck of the Golden Mary*, a shipwreck story whose interest was based on the dedication of the mate, written by Collins, to the noble captain, written by Dickens. The survival of the whole party depends on this relationship when, placed in the demanding setting of responsibility for the passengers and crew in two open boats following the wreck, the two men are challenged to act with the heroism Dickens had recognized in the characters of Franklin and Richardson. When Captain Ravender collapses under the strain, the mate takes over until the party is rescued.

The Wreck of the Golden Mary looked forward to *A Tale of Two Cities* not just in the relationship between two heroic men, but also in the heroine of the story, Lucy, a child with golden hair whose innocent vulnerability upholds them all when they drift at sea in the longboats after the wreck. She dies before they are rescued, but like Lucie Manette she acts as a spiritual guide to the hardened men in the boats.

The name "Lucy" for a golden-haired angelic female goes back for Dickens to his first love, little Lucy Stroughill, who lived next door to him at Ordnance Terrace when he was between the ages of five and nine.

While they were occupied with the Christmas story, Dickens and Collins were also engaged in another story of heroism and "manly friendship," this time a play, *The Frozen Deep*. Based on the Franklin story and set in the Arctic, the play transformed the Franklin-Richardson friendship into a rivalry over the love of one woman (just as *The Battle of Life* had been about two women in love with the same man, and the sacrifice of one of them for the other). Franklin's name was used for the good-hearted, noble Frank Aldersley, played by Wilkie Collins; Richardson became Richard Wardour, the unlikable and passionately jealous suitor whose beloved Clara Burnham has, we learn, turned her attention to the deserving Frank. Unknown to each other, the two men wind up together on an Arctic expedition and are eventually stranded together, at which point Wardour discovers that his companion is the hated rival on whom he has long ago sworn to take revenge. He could easily leave Frank to die, fulfilling the dream that he has brooded over for months. But when the time comes, his innate heroism rises to the fore and he carries the dying Aldersley to safety at the expense of his own life. In a final scene which took Victorian playgoers, even Queen Victoria, by storm, Wardour (played of course by Dickens), staggered on to the stage, laid the rescued Aldersley at the feet of their mutual love, and then died—reassured by the real tears of the actress who wept over his body that he had done the right thing and had received his reward. So completely did Dickens identify with the heroic Wardour that he "terrified Aldersley to that degree, by lunging at him to carry him into the cave, that the said Aldersley always shook like a mould of jelly, and muttered, 'This is an awful thing!'" (Nonesuch, 2:834). It was this experience, Dickens tells us, repeated night after night for a rapturous audience, that suggested Sydney Carton's sacrifice in *A Tale of Two Cities*.

In the preface to *A Tale of Two Cities*, Dickens tells us how important the acting of Richard Wardour was to his conception of Sydney Carton:

> When I was acting, with my children and friends, in Mr. Wilkie Collins's drama of The Frozen Deep, I first conceived the main idea of this story. A strong desire was upon me then, to embody it in my own person; and I traced out in my fancy, the state of mind of which it would necessitate the presentation to an observant spectator, with particular care and interest.
>
> As the idea became familiar to me, it gradually shaped itself into its present form. Throughout its execution, it has had the complete possession of me; I have so far verified what is done and suffered in these pages, as that I have certainly done and suffered it all myself.

"Done and suffered." Dickens did indeed suffer through the latter half of the 1850s. His identification with the unlikable, coarse, egotistical but ultimately heroic Richard Wardour had been an emotional release for him, and he wrote later to Collins that he had never had a moment's peace since the last night of the play. His letters of the time attest to his restless unhappiness, which he was able to forget in the play and which found expression in *A Tale of Two Cities*, the culmination of his interest in what a heroic man could do for a male friend. Although Carton and Wardour are inspired to save their rivals through the love of a woman, it is clear, especially in the novel, that the dying man considers that he is saving a friend.

Dickens and Collins replayed their roles as Wardour and Aldersley in real life, when in the autumn of 1857 they went on a walking tour in the Lake District. Collins, much the weaker of the two, sprained his ankle descending Carrock Fell and had to be carried down by Dickens, who made much of his heroic Wardour rescue in letters to friends. In the piece they wrote about the tour for *Household Words*, entitled *The Lazy Tour of Two Idle Apprentices*, Dickens, or Francis Goodchild, is feverishly energetic and active, in contrast to Collins, or Thomas Idle, who follows wearily behind his exuberant leader. The two sides of Sydney Carton, drunken idler and active hero, can be seen in these two roles.

A Tale of Two Cities was prefigured again in Dickens and Collins's 1857 Christmas story, The Perils of Certain English Prisoners. Again heroism was the theme, but Dickens was inspired this time, not by Sir John Franklin, but by the Cawnpore massacre in India, a revolt of a native army against its officers that resulted in the massacre of English men, women, and children. His intention was "to shadow out, in what I do the bravery of our ladies in India" (Nonesuch, 2:892). Dickens first used the name Carton in the story, and this Christmas story looks forward to A Tale of Two Cities in other ways as well.

The hero of The Perils of Certain English Prisoners is a private in the marines, Gill Davis, who at the beginning of the story is resentful of his lowly position and jealous of the gentlemen officers, including Captain George Carton. The heroine of the piece is Marion Maryon, who exemplifies the bravery of the women in India by fighting side by side with the men when pirates attack their silver mine in South America. Foreshadowing Lucie Manette and Sydney Carton, Marion is an unattainable angel who inspires Gill Davis to heroic action and saves him from further degradation. (The angelic heroine of The Battle of Life was also Marion.) Marion marries Captain Carton in the end, but remains the friend and protector of Davis. Davis is not called upon to sacrifice his life for Marion, but he is certainly prepared to do so, and he overcomes his jealous bitterness toward Captain Carton just as Wardour and Sydney do toward the rivals in their similar triangles. The redemption of an unlikable man by the love of an unattainable woman, placed in an exciting and dangerous setting, thus appeared twice in 1857 and was fully worked out in A Tale of Two Cities.

The French Revolution and the threat of the guillotine was a popular subject throughout the nineteenth century, and readers of A Tale of Two Cities have found echoes of it in a variety of other contemporary works. The most strikingly similar to A Tale of Two Cities is an obscure but at the time popular play, The Dead Heart, by Irish playwright Watts Phillips. Phillips had written his play three years earlier, but it did not appear until November 1859, three weeks before the conclusion of *A Tale of Two Cities* in *All the Year Round*. The similarities between the two caused the newspaper critics to shout "plagiarist!" of Phillips; so great was Dickens's reputation that the accusation was not made against him at the time, but later it has been suggested that Dickens borrowed, perhaps unconsciously, his plot and themes from the play. It is possible that he heard the play read by Benjamin Webster, the producer of the play and the actor of the hero's part, in 1857.[4]

There are certainly some striking similarities between *A Tale of Two Cities* and *The Dead Heart*. In the play the young hero, Landry, is imprisoned in the Bastille by an aristocrat who abducts his fiancée; thus like the Marquis, the aristocrat responsible for a rape is also responsible for an unjust imprisonment. Like Manette, Landry is released 18 years later, and in both works the phrases "buried alive" and "recalled to life" are used to describe their imprisonment. But the main similarity is one shared by other works of the time that dealt with the French Revolution: the substitution of the hero for someone else on the guillotine. In *The Dead Heart* Landry takes the place of his fiancée's son, whose death he has actually orchestrated because of the mother's apparent treachery. When he discovers at the last moment that he has been mistaken about her, his only redress is to die in the boy's place. The plot here resembles not only Sydney Carton's sacrifice, but also the way in which Dr. Manette's desire for vengeance against the Evrémonde family backfires on his daughter when his condemnation of his enemies and their ancestors condemns his son-in-law and Lucie's own child.

Phillips and Dickens had many mutual sources for the substitution idea, as it was a popular revolutionary motif. It had occurred in 1842 in Edward Bulwer Lytton's novel *Zanoni*, and more recently in *Le Chevalier de la Maison Rouge*, a play by Alexandre Dumas *père* that was produced in 1847. An English version of the play appeared in London in 1853. While *The Dead Heart* was playing at the Lyceum

Theatre, John Parselle's *The Changed Heart* was running at the nearby Surrey Theatre, and it too involved a substitution. All of these fictional sacrifices may have been based on an authentic anecdote in Thomas Carlyle's *French Revolution* (1837). Carlyle describes how Lieutenant-General Loiserolles substituted himself for his young son by answering to the death list while the boy was asleep.

Dickens no doubt knew *Zanoni,* written by his friend Bulwer Lytton, and he may have heard *The Dead Heart* read in 1857, the year of *The Frozen Deep.* But stories of substitutions on the guillotine and poor wretches "buried alive" in the Bastille were common property in writing about the Revolution. *A Tale of Two Cities* may have received some ideas from other sources, but the real inspiration for it was undoubtedly Dickens's own emotional upheaval in the years preceding it. The notion of the heroic in the everyday action and person had been the subject of *The Battle of Life;* in *The Frozen Deep* he was able to relieve some of his restless unhappiness by identifying with an unlikable hero who earns the love and respect of his rival and his love through self-sacrifice.

To add to his intense feelings about the role, he had fallen in love with Ellen Ternan, an 18-year-old actress who played the part of Lucy Crayford in the Manchester productions of *The Frozen Deep.* When the final break with his wife came in May 1858, there was some public talk about the cause; many friends knew about his relationship with Ellen, but there were also rumors that he was having an affair with Georgina, his unmarried sister-in-law who lived with the family and took over the role of mother to Dickens's children. Unfortunately Dickens overreacted violently to these rumors and made public statements about the breakup of the marriage in order to exonerate Ellen and Georgina. The publishing of *A Tale of Two Cities* was directly affected by the breakup, both in its emotional working out of guilt, expiation, and sacrifice, and in the form it took.

In 1850 Dickens had established his own weekly journal, *Household Words,* full of essays and stories by Dickens and other writers, as a means of coming into closer contact with his reading public. No writer has had a more personal relationship with his readers than did Dickens, and it meant more to him than almost any other relationship. It led to the public readings of his novels, the strain of which eventually killed him (these he began during the unhappy years of the 1850s too). By acting out his novels he could see their emotional effect on the audience and could revel in the power he had over such a wide variety of people, rich and poor, educated and simple. In a "Preliminary Word" to *Household Words* he stated his desire to "be the comrade and friend of many thousands of people, of both sexes, and of all ages and conditions, on whose faces we may never look." This desire to touch his public and be known by them was part of his satisfaction in playing Wardour in *The Frozen Deep*. He wrote to a friend that the play was "like writing a book in company; a satisfaction of a most singular kind, which has no exact parallel in my life" (Nonesuch, 2:825).

When Dickens issued a public statement about the breakup of his marriage, it appeared in the *Times* and other leading papers, but Bradbury and Evans, the publishers of *Household Words,* refused to publish it in their comic paper, *Punch.* Dickens took this refusal as a personal betrayal; he counted on the support of his publishers, who were a part of his very special relationship with his readers. He dissolved all his agreements with Bradbury and Evans, closing *Household Words* in May 1859 and beginning a new journal, *All the Year Round,* with his old publishers, Chapman and Hall, on 30 April.

In order to give *All the Year Round* a good start, he decided to write a serial for it, which would begin on 30 April and run in weekly parts until 26 November. The famous opening lines of *A Tale of Two Cities* thus launched the new journal and did indeed ensure its success: it sold a steady 100,000 copies each week. Chapman and Hall issued the novel in monthly parts as well, illustrated by Hablot Knight Browne (or "Phiz"), starting in June 1859. And so Dickens's personal revolution was brought before his public in a novel that explores the realms of public versus private, common good versus individual endeavour, universal noise versus private silence.

A Reading

5

The Setting:
Revolutionary France

"Whenever any reference (however slight) is made here to the condition of the French people before or during the Revolution, it is truly made, on the faith of trustworthy witnesses. It has been one of my hopes to add something to the popular and picturesque means of understanding that terrible time, though no one can hope to add anything to the philosophy of Mr. CARLYLE'S wonderful book" (xxvii). In his prefaces Dickens often felt called upon to justify the realistic details of his novels. He felt keenly that such details must be correct, and if challenged, as he frequently was, on the veracity of his references to factual events, he would respond in the preface to the first collected edition of the weekly or monthly parts. The most famous instance of such a response was in the preface to *Bleak House,* where he felt called upon to answer critics who had doubted that spontaneous combustion could really be the cause of Mr. Krook's death. Dickens replied: "I have no need to observe that I do not wilfully or negligently mislead my readers, and that, before I wrote that description, I took pains to investigate the subject."

Of all his subjects the revolutionary setting of *A Tale of Two Cities* was perhaps the one most requiring investigation, but there was no shortage of material for Dickens to draw on. By 1859 innumerable stories of suffering had emerged from diaries, memoirs, and other eye-witness accounts of the Terror; many others, like Doctor Manette's, were written in prison and stored away, never to see the light of day (how much better for Manette if his had suffered this fate instead of being recovered by the industrious Defarge and read out at Darnay's trial). These accounts provided firsthand evidence of the sufferings undergone by the victims of both the Terror and the ancien régime that preceded it.

As Dickens tells us, his main source of information on the Revolution was his friend Thomas Carlyle, whose epic three-volume account, *The French Revolution,* had appeared in 1837. After Dickens began *A Tale of Two Cities* in February 1859 he asked Carlyle to suggest background reading for him and was grateful, though probably somewhat overwhelmed, to receive "two cartloads" of books from the London Library.[1] He assured Carlyle that the books would give him the background he needed, adding, "if I should come to a knot in my planing, I shall come back to you to get over it" (Nonesuch, 2:97). Carlyle had himself done a formidable amount of research for his own study, and Dickens made use of some of the same sources, as he acknowledges in letters after *A Tale of Two Cities* was finished.

In reply to criticism of his portrayal of the aristocracy's treatment of the peasantry in eighteenth-century France, Dickens wrote at length to his friend Sir Edward Bulwer Lytton:

> In the first place, although the surrender of the feudal privileges (on a motion seconded by a nobleman of great rank) was the occasion of a sentimental scene, I see no reason to doubt, but on the contrary, many reasons to believe, that some of these privileges had been used to the frightful oppression of the peasant, quite as near to the time of the Revolution as the doctor's narrative, which, you will remember, dates long before the Terror. And surely when the new philosophy was the talk of the salons and the slang of the hour, it is not unreasonable or unallowable to suppose a nobleman wedded to the old cruel ideas, and representing the time going out, as his nephew represents the time coming in; as to the condition of the peasant in

The Setting: Revolutionary France

> France generally at that day, I take it that if anything be certain on earth it is certain that it was intolerable. . . .
>
> There is a curious book printed at Amsterdam, written to make out no case whatever, and tiresome enough in its literal dictionary-like minuteness, scattered up and down the pages of which is full authority for my marquis. This is Mercier's Tableau de Paris. Rousseau is the authority for the peasant's shutting up his house when he had a bit of meat. The tax-taker was the authority for the wretched creature's impoverishment. (Nonesuch, 2:162)

The Mercier book to which Dickens refers would have occupied quite a corner of the handcart, as it is actually 12 volumes, published in 1782–88. Dickens took many details of the Monseigneur's salon scene from Mercier: the number of servants required, the wearing of two watches by even the servants, the wealth of the Farmer-General, the description of the Convulsionists, and many of the other elements that make up his picture of a decadent, callous, and self-serving aristocracy.

Dickens cites Mercier as a source, and although he probably did consult the 12 volumes (in French) in his cartload, he would undoubtedly have had some of the details called to mind by an article that appeared in *Household Words* on 5 June 1858, its second part appearing on 19 June. Entitled "The Eve of the Revolution," it was written by Percy Fitzgerald, a friend of Dickens and one of his most prolific contributors. Fitzgerald's theme is the complacency of the aristocracy just before the storming of the Bastille; he marvels at their total blindness to the volcano that was boiling up beneath their feet and attributes this unconcern to the frivolous life that the aristocrats led. The operas, balls, and drunken revels that occupied the lives of the idle rich completely drowned out the rumblings of the volcano preparing for eruption.

We can see parallels between Fitzgerald's essays and *A Tale of Two Cities* in this volcanic metaphor, for Dickens too portrays the aristocracy as being too self-absorbed and self-satisfied to notice what was happening to the lower classes. Darnay's uncle the Marquis lives behind a stone mask, concerned only with keeping his place in the court circles and maintaining his pride and dignity as a member of an old noble family. Because he knows he is responsible for the deaths of three people and is guilty of all the charges of cruelty and inhumanity with which Darnay charges him at the château, he is like a volcano himself, full of pent-up rage and injured pride. Darnay reminds him that he has been out of favor with the court for years, as we know from the earlier scene when he is slighted at the Monseigneur's salon. His reaction to this slight is to lash out in fury when driving away, killing Gaspard's child with his wild coach. Fitzgerald also condemns this aristocratic practice and describes how fierce dogs often bounded in front, providing an equally dangerous hazard to the people on the street. According to Fitzgerald, the coach owner was responsible only if the front wheels caused the injury, and then he had to pay (but only if requested) a sum fixed by a tariff card at the police station.

Dickens's Marquis is clearly a more complex character than the aristocrats described by Fitzgerald; his disdain of Gaspard and his friends, whom he regards "as if they had been mere rats come out of their holes" (131), is caused not just by centuries of superiority but by injured pride that his own class has rejected him. But Fitzgerald's central image of the volcano building completely unseen and unheard by the nobility of France is present in *A Tale of Two Cities* in the footsteps heard by Lucie in Soho Square, miles away from the center of the volcano (or the storm, as Dickens refers to it). Dickens has been accused of heavy-handedness in his use of the footstep motif, which sounds a warning to the quiet household in London. But, like Fitzgerald, Dickens sees the upper classes in France as oblivious of the rising storm, wrapped up as they were in their own entertainments. In contrast the Manette family is sensitive to the rumblings because in the past they have been sensitive to the sufferings of the lower classes. Because of Doctor Manette's sympathy for the dying woman and her brother and Darnay's rejection of his family because of their cruelty to their tenants, the family in Soho have shown their awareness of the longstanding sufferings of the people and their sympathy with them. Like Dickens they fear the footsteps, and they know that they are dangerous simply because the upper classes are oblivious. Because the rumblings are ignored, the volcano has to erupt eventually. Dickens's message here for his contemporary readers was that an English volcano could be averted if the rumblings were responded to in time.

Another reference in Fitzgerald's essay was perhaps picked up by Dickens. Speaking again about "Paris sleeping unconsciously on the eve of eruption," Fitzgerald notes, "It is surprising in the midst of what gay, sprightly rioting and bacchanalian festivity that day of wrath surprised them. It was Belshazzar's feast over again, and the handwriting on the wall."[2] The biblical story has many interesting parallels for *A Tale of Two Cities* and is clearly behind Gaspard's writing of BLOOD on the wall with wine, when the cask spills in the first hint in the book of the troubles to come. Belshazzar's feast, a drunken revel for the king and his lords, was brought to an abrupt halt by the mysterious appearance of writing on the wall, which no one could interpret. Eventually Daniel was brought in, who explained to Belshazzar that the words were a warning. They told how Belshazzar's predecessor, Nebuchadnezzar, had been insufferably proud and overbearing as well as extravagant and wanton in his drunken parties. In punishment for setting himself up as a god, God deposed him, drove him out alone, turned his mind into that of a beast, and fed him grass. The parallel with Foulon is evident here. Belshazzar is accused by the writing on the wall of wantonness and pride; Daniel tells him that his kingdom has been brought to an end, that he has been "weighed in the balances and found wanting" (Daniel 5:27). In both bible story and novel, then, the writing on the wall signifies the end of the old order, an order characterized by drunkenness, luxury, and pride.

The Rousseau source to which Dickens refers in his letter was the *Confessions* (1782), an autobiography in which the philosopher Jean-Jacques Rousseau reiterated his influential beliefs: the corrupt nature of institutions, in fact the corruption of civilization in general; the superiority of the simple, uncivilized man (the "noble savage"); and the need for a democratic system to replace the authority of aristocracy and monarchy. Dickens, like other commentators on the Revolution, would have found in Rousseau's writings the prevailing discontent that fueled the events of 1789 and after. His specific reference to Rousseau as the source for a detail in Doctor Manette's letter is to Rousseau's description of dropping by a peasant's cottage to rest. The peasant gives him some simple food, but after a few minutes produces much better bread as well as ham, wine, and an omelette. He explains to Rousseau that he had feared that his unknown visitor was an excise man, who would have charged him duty on the bread and wine. Guessing that Rousseau was an "honest man" the peasant happily shared what he had with him. According to Rousseau, this evidence of the poor man's generosity in the face of intolerable burdens of taxation and deprivation instilled in him his "inextinguishable hatred . . . against the oppression to which these unhappy people are subject, and against their oppressors."[3] Dickens's version of the story is slightly different: Madame Defarge's dying brother speaks of hiding meat to prevent the Marquis's men from confiscating it.

As Dickens tells us in his preface, however, his main source of material for the factual events in the book was Carlyle's *The French Revolution*. He joked that he had read it 500 times (Forster, 2:57), and he carried it around with him when he was writing the novel. Dickens followed Carlyle closely, both in the chronology of the events of the Revolution and in his descriptions of the major historical scenes. He was selective, of course, in his portrayal of the Revolution, using only those scenes that bore upon his plot.

The storming of the Bastille is undoubtedly the most famous of all the events of the Revolution; it is still celebrated in France on 14 July because it was the beginning of the wave that was to sweep away all the old ways. The storming of the Bastille actually released only seven prisoners, as Dickens points out: four forgers, two madmen, and a follower of the Marquis de Sade; but the Bastille was the target of the first attack because for years it had housed innocent victims, like Doctor Manette, incarcerated often for years by the lettres de cachet that had allowed aristocrats to imprison enemies without trial. Its overthrow and subsequent tearing down symbolized the first chink in the armor of privilege and status.

The Setting: Revolutionary France

In describing the fall of the Bastille and its immediate results, Dickens relied on Carlyle for the sequence of events and for many details of the action and geographical layout (even though Carlyle admits that describing the siege "perhaps transcends the talent of mortals" and that even understanding the plan of the building is impossible after "infinite reading"[4]). Both accounts begin with the desperate search for arms, the mob being identified with Saint Antoine, the part of the city in which the attack takes place. Once armed, the mob becomes for Dickens a "living sea" (263), the relentless and mindless force that, once set in motion, cannot be turned back. The sea is first a "whirlpool of boiling waters" whose center point is Defarge's wine shop. Later Madame Defarge will remind the reader strongly of Lady Macbeth, and here Dickens recalls Shakespeare's play in his description of the whirlpool: "every human drop in the caldron had a tendency to be sucked towards the vortex where Defarge himself, already begrimed with gun-powder and sweat, issued orders, issued arms, thrust this man back, dragged this man forward, disarmed one to arm another, laboured and strove in the thickest of the uproar" (262). Carlyle had used this image also, describing minor whirlpools at every street barricade that "play distractedly into that grand Fire-Mahlstrom which is lashing round the Bastille" (FR, 1:200). Both accounts turn the initial whirlpool into a raging sea that sweeps all before it until, in Carlyle "rushes-in the living deluge: the Bastille is fallen!" (FR, 1:204).

In Dickens's description, as in all his historical scenes, the actions of his characters take center stage. Thus "the sea rose immeasurably wider and higher, and swept Defarge of the wine-shop over the lowered drawbridge, past the massive stone outer walls, in among the eight great towers surrendered! So resistless was the force of the ocean bearing him on, that even to draw his breath or turn his head was as impracticable as if he had been struggling in the surf at the South Sea" (264). Defarge is placed at the center of the maelstrom not only because his shop is the center of the revolutionary activity in Paris, but also because the Defarges are at the heart of Dickens's plot. From Manette's release in the first book to the final condemnation of Darnay in the last, the Defarges are there: silent witnesses at first; all too vocal witnesses at last. Defarge leads the "living sea" in its assault on the Bastille and, once inside, goes about his own secret business to find Doctor Manette's letter, which will later condemn Darnay.

The contents of the letter are not revealed until the trial; in fact there is no hint in the Bastille scene that Defarge has found anything. But here too the influence of *The French Revolution* is strong. In his description of the storming of the prison Carlyle writes:

> Likewise ashlar stones of the Bastille continue thundering through the dusk; its paper archives shall fly white. Old secrets come to view; and long-buried Despair finds voice. Read this portion of an old Letter: "If for my consolation Monseigneur would grant me, for the sake of God and the Most Blessed Trinity, that I could have news of my dear wife; were it only her name on a card, to show that she is alive! It were the greatest consolation I could receive; and I should for ever bless the greatness of Monseigneur". Poor Prisoner, who namest thyself *Quéret-Démery,* and hast no other history,—she is *dead,* that dear wife of thine, and thou art dead! 'Tis fifty years since thy breaking heart put this question; to be heard now first, and long heard, in the hearts of men. (*FR*, 1:207–8)

This is quite clearly the source of Manette's closing lines: "If it had pleased GOD to put it in the hard heart of either of the brothers, in all these frightful years, to grant me any tidings of my dearest wife— so much as to let me know by a word whether alive or dead—I might have thought that He had not quite abandoned them" (410).

Defarge's role as leader is quickly taken over by his wife, who in her silent watchful knitting is the novel's real center of the Terror. She takes center stage in the next historical scene, the murder of De Launay, the governor of the Bastille. Here too Dickens follows Carlyle, but makes his own character the central actor in the drama. Carlyle describes De Launay's attempt to take his own life, his appeal that they kill him fast, his decapitation, and the carrying of his head through the streets, "ghastly, aloft on a pike" (*FR*, 1:206). In the crowd's dogging of De Launay's footsteps Dickens adds the grim picture of Madame Defarge remaining "immovable close" to him (Dickens repeats the phrase five times) so that she can be the one to hew off his head once he is down, using her foot to steady his body. The horror of this description prepares the reader for Madame Defarge's implacable vengeance against Manette, Lucie, and her child at the end. While Defarge can show some humanity toward Darnay's family, his wife is marked here as given over to a machinelike resolve, one figure in "the remorseless sea of turbulently swaying shapes, voices of vengeance, and faces hardened in the furnaces of suffering until the touch of pity could make no mark on them" (268).

In the next historical scene, the murder of Foulon, Dickens again took his description from Carlyle, but added to it the intervention of the Defarges, the Vengeance, and Jacques Three. According to Carlyle, Joseph-Francois Foulon, a counsellor of state to Louis XVI and a man "grown grey in treachery, in griping, projecting, intriguing and iniquity," had proposed a harsh economic measure. To the question, "What will the people do?" he had replied publicly, "The people may eat grass" (*FR*, 1:117). Dickens includes Foulon's capture, hanging, and decapitation partly because it was a well-known event, but primarily because it was another instance of his "buried alive" theme, which we will be looking at in detail later. Fearing for his life, Foulon had faked his own death, mounting a lavish funeral (the body actually belonging to a servant) and going into hiding in the country. Like Roger Cly, he hoped to free himself from his prior and now dangerous identity by literally burying it and coming to life as another person. Although probably few aristocrats went to these lengths to escape the guillotine, certainly many, including the royal family, tried to escape by dressing as their servants. Dickens refers to this bitterly ironic downfall of the class who had often treated their servants as worse than dogs when the Monseigneur is forced to flee France in his cook's dress.

Carlyle describes how Foulon is taken to the Hotel de Ville for trial; how legal delay infuriates the republicans; how Lafayette is called in and wants to transfer Foulon to the Abbaye prison so that information about his accomplices may be "cunningly pumped out of him"; how at last someone urges, "What is the use of judging this man? Has he not been judged these thirty years?" (FR, 1:215–16). Dickens's description includes the delay, adding Madame Defarge as an eye-witness, passing out a running commentary to the impatient mob waiting outside. But instead of the appeal that Foulon has already been judged, Dickens gives a more abstruse reason for the mob's overthrow of "justice": "At length the sun rose so high that it struck a kindly ray as of hope or protection, directly down upon the old prisoner's head. The favour was too much to bear; in an instant the barrier of dust and chaff that had stood surprisingly long, went to the winds, and Saint Antoine had got him!" (274). There is an element of sympathy for Foulon in Dickens's description, felt by Dickens rather than by the Defarges and their friends, who would hardly have seen the ray of light on Foulon's head as a "kindly ray" suggesting some sort of divine sympathy with the old man. It was perhaps Foulon's age and infirmity that inspired a sort of sympathy in Dickens, who describes Madame Defarge's enjoyment of his long drawn out hanging as that of a cat playing with a mouse. When the rope eventually breaks, Dickens describes it as "merciful" (275).

Carlyle too is appalled by the brutality of the revenge against Foulon, describing him as "the pitiablest, most unpitied of all old men" (FR 1:215). The turning of the tables here, when the people he had said could eat grass now stuff grass into his dead mouth, is feared by both Dickens and Carlyle as epitomizing what was most disturbing about the course of the Revolution: the more oppressed a people are, the more violent and brutal will be their rebellion when it comes; and the injustices and wrongs that caused the revolution will be adopted by the new ruling class—the oppressed become the oppressors in their turn. Madame Defarge can no more differentiate between Darnay and his Marquis uncle than the Marquis could regard the servant class as being made up of individuals with individual worth. Both see people in terms only of class, to be judged mechanically as a group. Thus Carlyle writes of Foulon's death with some misgivings: "Surely if Revenge is a 'kind of justice,' it is a 'wild' kind! . . . They that would make grass be eaten do now eat grass, in *this* manner? After long dumb-groaning generations, has the turn suddenly become thine?—To such abysmal overturns . . . are human Solecisms all liable, if they but knew it; the more liable, the falser (and topheavier) they are!" (*FR*, 1:216).

The violence and horror of the revolutionary scenes increase with the growing tension and suspense of the novel's plot. The deaths of De Launay, Foulon, and later Foulon's son-in-law, and Madame Defarge's pitiless enjoyment of them, are graphically depicted and frighteningly vivid. But more horrifying still is "The Grindstone," chapter 2 of the third book. Now the mob's thirst for vengeance is totally out of control. Dickens deliberately set Darnay's return to Paris and arrest at the time of the September Massacres, a four-day execution of 1,089 prisoners from four Paris prisons, condemned in minutes each by what Carlyle refers to as "sudden Courts of Wild-Justice" (*FR*, 2:150). Again Dickens took the main details of his description from Carlyle, but builds up the grindstone metaphor and places the grindstone itself outside the Paris office of Tellson's, the English bank, to emphasize the juxtaposition of the Manette family versus the revolutionaries, love versus hate, peace versus turmoil, protection versus destruction that figures so largely in the third part of the novel. Part of the horror of the grindstone image is its metaphorical force: a relentless, implacable machine, it recalls the beanstalk giant who was going to grind Jack's bones to make his bread. It is always associated with Hell, the greater setting of the whole scene in both Carlyle and Dickens. In Carlyle we read: "And another sinks, and another; and there forms itself a piled heap of corpses, and the kennels begin to run red. Fancy the yells of these men, their faces of sweat and blood; the crueller shrieks of these women, for there are women too. . . . Man after man is cut down; the sabres need sharpening, the killers refresh themselves from wine-jugs. Onward and onward goes the butchery; the loud yells wearying down into bass growls" (*FR*, 2:151).

Dickens's grindstone scene exemplifies perhaps more obviously Carlyle's prefatory remark that "there are depths in man that go the length of lowest Hell" (*FR*, 2:148): Dickens writes, "Their hideous countenances were all bloody and sweaty, and all awry with howling, and all staring and glaring with beastly excitement and want of sleep. As these ruffians turned and turned, their matted locks now flung forward over their eyes, now flung backward over their necks, some women held wine to their mouths that they might drink; and what with dropping blood, and what with dropping wine, and what with the stream of sparks struck out of the stone, all their wicked atmosphere seemed gore and fire" (321). Dickens's sympathy with the revolutionaries has all but disappeared by this scene, as he makes clear at the end of it when he describes the "frenzied eyes" of the mad workers at the grindstone: "eyes which any unbrutalised beholder would have given twenty years of life, to petrify with a well-directed gun" (322).

But Dickens has made clear as the novel progresses that these wild murderers are scarcely human now; they are already petrified, "changed into wild beasts, by terrible enchantment long persisted in" (286). The enchantment is the centuries of oppression by the Marquis and his class, who have taxed and starved the peasant class until, now roused, they are no longer human but mechanical, driven robots. Monseigneur, Dickens says, as a member of the upper class, is "like the fabled rustic who raised the Devil with infinite pains, and was so terrified at the sight of him that he could ask the Enemy no question, but immediately fled" (286).

In his dramatic depiction of the historic scenes of the novel Dickens, like Carlyle, took a romantic approach to history, bringing it to life for the reader in a way that was new to nineteenth-century readers. One historian's assessment of this new approach describes exactly Dickens's success in the writing of history: "The Romantic movement aimed at a new history, narrative, live, picturesque, direct, full of particular detail and local colour, alive with the touch and the atmosphere of the past, populated by individual characters, a history which is artistically effective, written through artistic identification and creating a sense of emotional identification in the reader."[5] In all of these ways Dickens built upon Carlyle's foundation but formed the historical scenes into his own dramatic story.

6

The Setting:
England

Nearly all of book 1 of *A Tale of Two Cities* takes place in England; all of book 3 takes place in France. The shift from one to the other is both alternating and gradual: the first four chapters take place in England, and the next two, completing book 1, take place in France; the first six chapters of book 2 are in England, and the next three in France, then five in England and two in France. As the threads of the two stories start to come together with Lucie's wedding, Doctor Manette's mental relapse, and Carton's declaration of love to Lucie, four English chapters are followed by "Echoing Footsteps" (chapter 21), which begins in England but ends in France, the link between the countries being the realization in Saint Antoine of the footsteps heard more and more urgently by Lucie in Soho. After two French chapters, book 2 ends with one London chapter, but it is a London drawn into the happenings across the channel by the rush of aristocrats fleeing to the safety of Tellson's Bank. From this safety Darnay is drawn "to the loadstone rock" of Paris.

As the English scenes gradually give way to the French ones, we can see Dickens's attitude to the England of the late eighteenth century changing also. At the beginning of the novel Dickens paints a grim picture of both countries. They both had kings who believed in their divine right to rule. English spirituality had deteriorated into communing with spirits and other superstitious practices (Dickens deplored this about the contemporary scene also, in his 1859 Christmas story *The Haunted House,* which debunked spirit rapping and ghost stories). France, he says, was less given over to such spiritual revelations, but had instead a clergy that inflicted cruel punishments for minor offenses. In England, lawlessness went hand in hand with a barbarous justice system that hanged murderers and petty thieves alike. Both crime and punishment were marked by cruelty and violence, while the kings of both countries "carried their divine rights with a high hand" (4).

The lawlessness described in the opening chapter is realized in the next, when the metaphorical road of the plot opens before us as a dark, fog-bound, muddy, and treacherous climb up Shooter's Hill, infamous haunt of highwaymen. So forbidding is the scene, hell-like in the intensity of the "steaming mist" that envelops the travelers like "the waves of an unwholesome sea" (6), that it is no surprise when a highwayman does loom out of the fog. It turns out to be Jerry with a message for Mr. Lorry, but the reply to the message is so cryptic— "Recalled to life"—that the mystery surrounding the coach and its passengers is only deepened by it. In his opening description of England's lawlessness Dickens has already mentioned the ubiquitous highwayman, dangerous robber by night, "city tradesman in the light" (3), just as Jerry himself is a grave robber by night, a messenger for respectable Tellson's by day. Both are dual personalities, living a double life.

Dickens's opening comparison of the two countries refers to the royal courts' resistance to change, because the status quo was eminently suited to those holding power and position: "In both countries it was clearer than crystal to the lords of the State preserves of loaves and fishes, that things in general were settled for ever" (1). This blindness to the lawlessness and violence that were a part of serious social unrest is symptomatic of the laissez-faire system of government that Dickens is attacking in the novel.

The Setting: England

Equally opposed to change at the beginning of the novel is Tellson's Bank, symbol of British economic and cultural security and solidity. As Jarvis Lorry reflects on Tellson's underground strong rooms, he finds them "safe, and strong, and sound, and still, just as he had last seen them" (15). But Mr. Lorry, on his way to dig Doctor Manette out of a living grave, finds in his troubled dreams that Tellson's underground safes merge with Manette's plight to become a grave also; he cannot prevent his mind from sliding away "into the bank and the grave" (16). And if graves can be dug up and plundered (and Jerry the messenger hints that he does just that) could not Tellson's be similarly desecrated?

At the beginning of the novel Tellson's and Mr. Lorry are both seen as a part of the ancien régime, the status quo that prefers to remain oblivious of the volcanic rumblings around it. Tellson's is "very small, very dark, very ugly, very incommodious," and old-fashioned also in its partners' pride in these attributes. Dickens likens the old bankers to the British government, "which did very often disinherit its sons for suggesting improvements in laws and customs that had long been highly objectionable, but were only the more respectable" (59). Dickens reminded his contemporary readers of parallels between Tellson's and the ancien régime in France in his choice of the bank's name: Thelusson's was a French bank made famous by one of its former employees, Jacques Necker, who as minister of finance tried to institute financial reforms. His dismissal by Louis XVI was one of the immediate causes of the storming of the Bastille.

Dickens's characteristic humor is most in evidence (and of all his novels, *A Tale of Two Cities* is the least humorous) in his description of banking at Tellson's, which he likens, appropriately for the plot, to being in jail: "If your business necessitated your seeing 'the House,' you were put into a species of Condemned Hold at the back." Even if you were released in time, your possessions and bank notes were stored there as though in a grave, acquiring "a musty odour, as if they were fast decomposing into rags again" (60). With its iron bars at the windows, its dank vaults and massive keys, Tellson's Bank resembles the Bastille. Its vaults even contain buried letters, grim foreshadowing of Doctor Manette's hidden testimony: "Your lighter boxes of family papers went up-stairs . . . where, even in the year one thousand seven hundred and eighty, the first letters written to you by your old love, or by your little children, were but newly released from the horror of being ogled through the windows, by the heads exposed on Temple Bar" (60). In this comparison Dickens is suggesting that if the Bastille could fall to an attack, so could Tellson's.

Dickens even associates Tellson's with the inhuman justice system, as the bank has been responsible for putting to death forgers, coiners, petty thieves, horse thieves, even "the unlawful opener of a letter" (61). Dickens argues that, far from preventing crime, such brutality actually has the opposite effect. There are many echoes here of the brutality to come in the Revolution. Tellson's lies in the shadow of Temple Bar, a large stone gateway (now perched incongruously in a field outside London), which up till 1780 held the decapitated heads of executed criminals. Such exhibitions were commonplace in the Terror, as we see with De Launay and Foulon. Dickens remarks sarcastically that the only benefit of capital punishment on such a large scale was that "it cleared off (as to this world) the trouble of each particular case, and left nothing else connected with it to be looked after" (61), just as the revolutionaries were careless about which heads fell victim to the guillotine. As the little seamstress says to Carton, will her death really help the cause of the Revolution?

Tellson's made sure that its new members were trained in the old ways, as youth is notoriously given to reform; any young man was hidden away "in a dark place, like a cheese, until he had the full Tellson flavour and blue-mould upon him" (61). Tellson's employees could be said to be "buried alive" also. In these early scenes Mr. Lorry appears as very much a product of Tellson's Bank: old, dependable, set in his ways, unimaginative, businesslike. He refuses to be led into any emotional disclosure, falling back repeatedly on his assertion that he has "no feelings" but is a "mere machine" (26). It is clear even now, however, that this mechanical exterior is the product of Tellson's rigid training in "business." Mr. Lorry's "face habitually suppressed and quieted, was still lighted up under the quaint wig by a pair of moist bright eyes that it must have cost their owner, in years gone by, some pains to drill to the composed and reserved expression of Tellson's Bank" (20). Like Wemmick in *Great Expectations,* Mr. Lorry comes to lead a double life, one involving the hard-hearted business exterior for the office, the other the kindly and loving interior for the family. Mr. Lorry has had no need of his inner self until the family at Soho Square adopts him as a kind of uncle and adviser.

Dickens makes clear that Mr. Lorry's "business absorption" is a kind of disease or aberration, rather like Doctor Manette's absorption in shoe making, because, like Manette, Lorry suffers "several relapses" (108) into business before becoming the doctor's friend. By the end of the novel Mr. Lorry has achieved a kind of heroic stature in his loyal and stalwart devotion to the Manette family. His mental habit remains with him, as he tells Carton near the end that he "was a man of business when a boy" (383), but Carton recognizes how much more than a man of business Mr. Lorry is and tells him "I could not respect your sorrow more, if you were my father" (381). Mr. Lorry's transformation from a repressed, reserved banker to an active and compassionate friend is part of the movement that takes place in the novel in the depiction of England.

England comes out very badly at Darnay's Old Bailey trial. Like Tellson's, the London court of law is old-fashioned, rooted in the old ways, and resistant to change. Dickens frequently attacked people who fondly remembered the "good old days," and here he reminds us of the barbaric justice system of those old days, which is still in evidence in 1780:

> For the rest, the Old Bailey was famous as a kind of deadly inn-yard, from which pale travellers set out continually, in carts and coaches, on a violent passage into the other world: traversing some two miles and a half of public street and road, and shaming few good citizens, if any. So powerful is use, and so desirable to be good use in the beginning. It was famous, too, for the pillory, a wise old institution, that inflicted a punishment of which no one could foresee the extent; also, for the whipping-post, another dear old institution, very humanising and softening to behold in action; also, for

extensive transactions in blood-money, another fragment of ancestral wisdom, systematically leading to the most frightful mercenary crimes that could be committed under Heaven. Altogether, the Old Bailey, at that date, was a choice illustration of the precept, that "Whatever is is right;" an aphorism that would be as final as it is lazy, did it not include the troublesome consequence, that nothing that ever was, was wrong. (69)

Dickens is juxtaposing here Britain's ancien régime with both the ancien régime of France and the new régime of Revolutionary France, as we can see the obvious foreshadowing of the French Revolution in the "violent passage" of the accused from their trials at the Old Bailey to their executions at Tyburn and later Newgate. Their journey of two miles and a half, where they are exposed to public ridicule and condemnation before the barbarity of a public execution, reminds us forcibly of Carton's last journey to the guillotine on the tumbril with the little seamstress. At the same time Dickens is attacking the contemporary economic system of laissez-faire in his reference to Alexander Pope's phrase, "Whatever is, is right." The Monseigneur too had "one truly noble idea of general public business, which was, to let everything go on in its own way" (124). Carlyle and Dickens both saw this attitude as detrimental to political or social reform; it suited the ruling class to keep things as they were. But like the aristocrats in France dancing on a volcano, the British aristocracy may actually have had much to fear from such complacency.

Darnay's trial, attended by a "tainted crowd," described as a "hideous scene of action," is a travesty of justice and common human decency. Accused of treachery, Darnay faces the most brutal of punishments, hanging, drawing, and quartering, and Dickens was relying here on a real case. In his review of *A Tale of Two Cities*, Sir James Fitzjames Stephen drew attention to the similarity between Darnay's trial and that of a French spy, De la Motte, who was tried for treason in 1781 and sentenced to death. Dickens would have known about De la Motte's trial through the *Annual Register*, in which it was reported. As in Darnay's trial, the prosecution's case rested on the evidence of an informer, but there was no Sydney Carton to undermine the identification of the accused. Stephen considered the De la Motte trial admirably fair, and Dickens's version a malicious swipe at the British judicial system.

Dickens attacks both the bloodthirstiness of the audience and the faults of a justice system that could give such credibility to obviously trumped up crown witnesses; on both counts he is foreshadowing the French trials of Darnay in book 3. When Jerry asks the man beside him about the case, the man tells him "with a relish" about the brutality of the punishment and assures Jerry that the accused will be found guilty, "don't you be afraid of that" (70). When Darnay is brought in, he is very clearly one against the mob, as he and his few friends are later in revolutionary Paris. At the trial we see the first chilling instance of the private man held up to public observation and humiliation, as will happen to so many victims of the Terror:

> Everybody present, except the one wigged gentleman [Carton] who looked at the ceiling, stared at him. All the human breath in the place, rolled at him, like a sea, or a wind, or a fire. Eager faces strained round pillars and corners, to get a sight of him; spectators in back rows stood up, not to miss a hair of him; people on the floor of the court, laid their hands on the shoulders of the people before them, to help themselves, at anybody's cost, to a view of him—stood a-tiptoe, got upon ledges, stood upon next to nothing, to see every inch of him. Conspicuous among these latter, like an animated bit of the spiked wall of Newgate, Jerry stood. (71)

We see this same brutal fascination at the deaths of De Launay, Foulon, and the other victims of the Revolution, and Dickens foreshadows the French deaths through his image of the human breath rolling at Darnay "like a sea, or a wind, or a fire." These three elemental forces are the ones he uses to describe the revolutionaries in action. Dickens emphasizes that it is the severity of the punishment that attracts this "Ogreish" interest: "The form that was to be doomed to be so shamefully mangled, was the sight; the immortal creature that was to be so butchered and torn asunder, yielded the sensation" (72). Here, in peaceful England, we have the same ghoulish pleasure that Madame

Defarge and her fellow knitters take in watching the bloody heads fall into the sack at the guillotine.

The courtroom scene makes clear the separation between the accused and the audience, including the judge; he is separated from them by the dock and by the herbs spread there to prevent prison fever, brought in by the accused, from infecting the rest of the court. This separation is the subject of Dickens's next novel, *Great Expectations*, in which the hero Pip learns that we cannot separate ourselves from others who, often through no real fault of their own, end up in the criminal dock. Pip spends most of the novel trying to free himself from his criminal connections, only to find that the woman he loves is a criminal's daughter, and his benefactor is that criminal. In the trial scene, Pip holds Magwitch's hand and acknowledges his responsibility to care for him to the end.

Darnay's trial itself is a brilliant example of Dickens's style, as the defense reveals that the chief crown witness is a liar and a crook, the whole dialogue told through indirect reported speech: "Ever been in prison? Certainly not. Never in a debtors' prison?—Come, once again. Never? Yes. How many times? Two or three times. Not five or six? Perhaps. Of what profession? Gentleman. Ever been kicked? Might have been. Frequently? No. Ever kicked down stairs? Decidedly not; once received a kick on the top of a staircase, and fell down stairs of his own accord. Kicked on that occasion for cheating at dice? Something to that effect was said by the intoxicated liar who committed the assault, but it was not true" (78). The evidence of both John Barsad and Roger Cly, while clearly invented for their own ends, is still going to condemn Darnay in this court of injustice, until Carton calmly casts doubt on the important question of identification. At the acquittal of the prisoner the "baffled blue-flies" are left searching for "other carrion" (91).

Dickens's purpose in his opening chapter is to show the similarities between France under the ancien régime and England of the 1780s. But his descriptions of Darnay's trial and the injustices of Tellson's Bank prefigure the atrocities of the Revolution more than the cruelties of the ancien régime, partly because most of the novel takes place in Revolutionary France. Dickens's portrayal of the ancien régime is seen chiefly at the Monseigneur's salon, at Evrémonde's château in the conversation between the Marquis and Darnay, and in retrospect through Doctor Manette's testimony. The gruesome punishment for treason does recall the threatened punishment to Gaspard, however, which a villager describes in horrific detail, concluding that "all this was actually done to a prisoner who made an attempt on the life of the late King, Louis Fifteen. But how do I know if he lies? I am not a scholar" (205). The old man was not lying, as such a punishment befell Robert François Damiens for attempting to stab the King. Dickens would have read of the torture in Mercier. The ancien régime was guilty of many other atrocities also committed by the English, according to Dickens's opening, such as imprisoning people without trial, but the main points of comparison are with the France of the Revolution, Dickens's point being that the cruelties of the oppressive former age give rise to an equally cruel and unjust reaction.

After the trial the scenes shift to France, the only English setting now being the Manettes' peaceful house in Soho. From the opening descriptions of England as a country similar to France in its lawlessness, barbarity of crime and punishment, and injustice in law, England is now seen as everything France is not. The Soho scenes alternate with the French ones, not for comparison, but for contrast. Madame Defarge's implacable knitting of names into her register that will condemn the named to the guillotine is contrasted with Lucie's simple but decorative and homely housekeeping. The Defarges do not seem to have a home; we see them always in their place of business, the wine shop, which is not even a friendly gathering place but a sinister cover for revolutionary plots. While Madame Defarge wears a flower solely as a secret code to the revolutionaries, Lucie tends flowers for their beauty and naturalness.

The Monseigneur's salon is contrasted with Soho also, in its artificial and uncomfortable extravagance, and the "leprosy of unreality" that "disfigured" (126) the servile followers of Monseigneur. The women in the salon do not own to being mothers; having brought a "troublesome creature" (126) into the world, these aristocratic women hand their babies over to peasant women to bring up. Madame Defarge is childless; Lucie of course is above all an exemplary mother. The Evrémondes' château is contrasted with Lucie's house also, as the scene of a vicious rape of a pregnant, married woman. The château itself is the very antithesis of a home, "a stony business altogether" (141) like its owner.

Just as the house in Soho Square becomes a refuge from the world, sought out by Darnay, Carton, and Mr. Lorry, so Tellson's Bank becomes a refuge for émigrés fleeing from Revolutionary France in the third part of the novel. At first this connection accords with the opening description of the Bank as a rather contemptible adjunct of the ancien régime of both countries: the émigrés who take refuge there are arrogant, cowardly rakes, desperately trying to hold on to the old social system that had benefited them so much, and boastful that they can avenge themselves on the revolutionaries before long. It is their condemnation of the anonymous Marquis St. Evrémonde (Darnay himself) that sends Darnay back to France to help poor Gabelle, his old servant, and to try to do something for the "ruffian herd," as one émigré calls the peasants on Evrémonde's land. Stryver, Darnay's counsel at the trial, represents the old school of Englishman who agrees with the émigrés that the revolutionaries are "the vilest scum of the earth that ever did murder by wholesale" (293). The émigrés and "native British orthodoxy" agree that the Revolution is

> the one only harvest ever known under the skies that had not been sown—as if nothing had ever been done, or omitted to be done, that had led to it—as if observers of the wretched millions in France, and of the misused and perverted resources that should have made them prosperous, had not seen it inevitably coming, years before, and had not in plain words recorded what they saw. Such vapouring, combined with the extravagant plots of Monseigneur for the restoration of a state of things that had utterly exhausted itself, and worn out Heaven and earth as well as itself, was hard to be endured without some remonstrance by any sane man who knew the truth. (291)

The Setting: England

By the time Dickens has been swept up in the Terror, however, his sympathy with the revolutionaries has been tempered by the viciousness and mindlessness of their revenge against the aristocracy. He never fails to see that the Terror was the result of the "frightful moral disorder, born of unspeakable suffering, intolerable oppression, and heartless indifference" (428), but at the same time he adopts a new tone when talking about the revolutionaries. We have already seen how "a well-directed gun" would not be out of place in dealing with the mob around the grindstone, and even the servants of the Monseigneur come in for the sort of ironic treatment that their master received in the earlier salon scene: "Monseigneur gone, and the three strong men absolving themselves from the sin of having drawn his high wages, by being more than ready and willing to cut his throat on the altar of the dawning Republic one and indivisible of Liberty, Equality, Fraternity, or Death, Monseigneur's house had been first sequestrated, and then confiscated" (316). Nowhere before has Dickens suggested that the aristocrats actually paid "high wages." When Tellson's takes over the Monseigneur's house, it becomes, not an escape for arrogant and cowardly aristocrats, but a haven in the midst of a world gone mad with the thirst for blood. The grindstone is set up outside it, and Mr. Lorry can hear beyond the walls a hum with an "indescribable ring in it, weird and unearthly, as if some unwonted sounds of a terrible nature were going up to Heaven" (318). Tellson's Bank is a sandbar in the turbulent ocean. Similarly England represents safety and sanity; the Manettes, Mr. Lorry, and Charles Darnay flee for their lives through the barriers of Paris and northern France to their home across the water. No suggestion now of highwaymen on the Dover Road, corrupt witnesses, or barbaric punishments.

The shift in Dickens's attitude toward England can be seen most clearly in the development of Miss Pross. This indomitable lady is a fearsome figure, a noisy but comic Madame Defarge, when we first encounter her through Mr. Lorry's eyes at Dover:

A wild-looking woman, whom even in his agitation, Mr. Lorry observed to be all of a red colour, and to have red hair, and to be dressed in some extraordinary tight-fitting fashion, and to have on her head a most wonderful bonnet like a Grenadier wooden measure, and good measure too, or a great Stilton cheese, came running into the room in advance of the inn servants, and soon settled the question of his detachment from the poor young lady, by laying a brawny hand upon his chest, and sending him flying back against the nearest wall.

("I really think this must be a man!" was Mr. Lorry's breathless reflection, simultaneously with his coming against the wall.) (30)

Miss Pross's strength in this scene is of course a preparation for her final confrontation with Madame Defarge. In both scenes her unusual ferocity is aroused, as a female tiger's would be, by an apparent threat to her young, Lucie Manette. And like an animal (or a mother), she is both strong to the death against the attacker and contrastingly tender to the child in her care, tending Lucie "with great skill and gentleness" (31).

Miss Pross is in many ways a counterpart to Mr. Lorry, and they have several exchanges in the book. Both are unmarried, both set in their ways, both unmistakably English in their attitudes. Their names are good solid Anglo-Saxon ones. At the beginning, both Mr. Lorry and Miss Pross are seen as narrowly English, provincial and unimaginative as the stereotype holds. (In a Christmas story for *All the Year Round* called "His Boots," Dickens actually calls a character Mr. the Englishman from a French misunderstanding of his real name, Mr. Langley, or Mr. "L'Anglais," and characterizes him as stuffy, emotionally rigid, and unable at first to unleash the pent-up humanity and compassion that he has buried over the years.) When Mr. Lorry asks Miss Pross how she imagines Doctor Manette's mental state to be, she begins by declaring, "Never imagine anything. Have no imagination at all" (114). Miss Pross prides herself on this attribute, just as Mr. Lorry has depended on his assertion that he is a mechanical businessman.

But in this scene in which they discuss Doctor Manette's imprisonment, both show themselves to be quite the opposite of the exterior they like to present. When Miss Pross describes how in the dead of night Doctor Manette can be heard "walking up and down," and how Lucie has learnt that then "his mind is walking up and down, walking up and down, in his old prison" (115), Dickens notes that "there was a perception of the pain of being monotonously haunted by one sad idea, in her repetition of the phrase, walking up and down, which testified to her possessing" (116) a particularly perceptive imagination. When Mr. Lorry asks her why Doctor Manette never talks about the reason for his imprisonment, or the identity of his oppressors, she replies that as the imprisonment was the cause of his losing himself, he probably fears that the recollection of it could cause him to lose himself again. Mr. Lorry considers this a "profounder remark" than he had expected and demonstrates his own perceptiveness when he replies that such suppression may be harmful. It is fitting that Mr. Lorry and Miss Pross are responsible for the "murder" of the Doctor's workbench, the relic and mental crutch of his years of imprisonment, for both are sensitive to its place in the doctor's mental stability.

Gradually Mr. Lorry and Miss Pross are shown to be softening under the good influence of Lucie and her family, so that by the third part they are no longer stereotypes of an old England of which Dickens is critical. Dickens's fear of the mechanistic view of human life and society at first noticeable in the depiction of Tellson's Bank, Mr. Lorry, and Miss Pross is gradually transferred to the revolutionaries. We see it in Madame Defarge's knitting, in her husband's mechanical way of speaking, in the uniform appearance of the Jacquerie, in the insistence on sameness in the term "Citizen," and in the inexorable mechanism of the guillotine itself.

Just as inexorable is Madame Defarge's pursuit of Darnay and his relatives. She is no longer a woman: "imbued from her childhood with a brooding sense of wrong, and an inveterate hatred of a class, opportunity had developed her into a tigress. She was absolutely without pity" (447). As she makes her way to the Manettes' lodgings, the use of the repeated phrase "still, Madame Defarge, pursuing her way along the streets, came nearer and nearer" (450) reminds us that she is like a machine in her determination to avenge her sister's murder. Against such mechanism the dynamic characters in the book are pitted, and we see it graphically in the struggle between Miss Pross and Madame Defarge. Both are single-minded and powerful through their intense feelings. But whereas Miss Pross is motivated by love, a dynamic force, Madame Defarge is governed by a blind desire for revenge, so overwhelming that "it was nothing to her, that an innocent man was to die for the sins of his forefathers; she saw, not him, but them. It was nothing to her, that his wife was to be made a widow and his daughter an orphan; that was insufficient punishment, because they were her natural enemies and her prey, and as such had no right to live" (447).

In the final confrontation, Miss Pross's Englishness again is central to her characterization, but now it is seen not as a joke but as an asset. Although the shooting of Madame Defarge is accidental, Miss Pross has had the upper hand throughout because she is more imaginative (her tears of courage are mistaken by Madame Defarge for tears of weakness—Madame Defarge typically underestimates her) and because she fights with "the vigorous tenacity of love, always so much stronger than hate" (455). Neither understands the other's language, but both comprehend much of what the other is saying—the scene is very much the confrontation of two animals who communicate nonverbally through the language of love, hate, power, and desire. But it is a victory for British love against foreign hate: Madame Defarge "shall not get the better of me. I am an Englishwoman" (453), declares Miss Pross. There is a certain amount of "Rule Britannia" ("Britons never never never shall be slaves"—Dickens makes fun of this anthem quite frequently in his writing) in Miss Pross's patriotism, but Dickens is reassuring his readers that the British working class is different from the French and that Tellson's Bank, for all its institutional drawbacks, will never be guilty of the atrocities of the French émigrés because beneath its business exterior beats the heart of Mr. Lorry.

Dickens's patriotism at the end of the book could be considered too heavily chauvinistic were it not for the leavening effect of the spy Barsad. That Miss Pross's brother (about whom she is eternally blind) and his coconspirator Roger Cly are as British as Lorry and Carton, but are unredeemably selfish, cowardly, and dishonest makes more acceptable Dickens's otherwise one-sided view of the British in France. For all Madame Defarge's frightening similarity to a tormented beast, she cannot be accused of any of the petty vices. Barsad, in contrast, is a weasel rather than a tiger; he does not have to earn his living as a spy.

It is entirely fitting that Madame Defarge should suffer an accidental death at the hands of Miss Pross. We can see from the Dover scene with Mr. Lorry that the two women are one of the many doublings in the book, set on different roads but fated to meet before the journey is done. Dickens explains this rightness himself in a letter to Edward Bulwer Lytton:

> I am not clear, and I never have been clear, respecting that canon of fiction which forbids the interposition of accident in such a case as Madame Defarge's death. Where the accident is inseparable from the passion and emotion of the character, where it is strictly consistent with the whole design, and arises out of some culminating proceeding on the part of the character which the whole story has led up to, it seems to me to become, as it were, an act of divine justice. And when I use Miss Pross (though this is quite another question) to bring about that catastrophe, I have the positive intention of making that half-comic intervention a part of the desperate woman's failure, and of opposing that mean death—instead of a desperate one in the streets, which she wouldn't have minded—to the dignity of Carton's wrong or right; this *was* the design, and seemed to be in the fitness of things. (Nonesuch, 3:162–63).

7

"Reading in Teaspoons": The Plot

When Dickens, annoyed with his publishers, decided to close his old weekly journal *Household Words* and start a new one, *All the Year Round,* he had the perfect vehicle for the new story he had been turning over in his mind since his acting in *The Frozen Deep.* The new journal needed a strong serial to get the buying public interested in it; what could be better than a stirring tale about the French Revolution?

Although most of Dickens's novels were published in monthly numbers of 32 pages, he had published in weekly numbers before: *The Old Curiosity Shop* and *Barnaby Rudge* (1840–41) in *Master Humphrey's Clock* and *Hard Times* (1854) in *Household Words.* While writing these earlier novels he complained bitterly about the constraints of the weekly form; although he chose magazine publication because it would bring him closer to his reading public, it did not suit his expansive style, and he found himself wanting "elbow-room terribly" (Forster, 1:143). He feared that his readers would be impatient to know more than he could tell them each week, but mostly he felt his wings clipped by having to condense character development and the creation of atmosphere and symbolic background. As well, the weekly form required some sort of minor suspense at the end of each small section to bring the readers back for more. He handled the writing of weekly installments very successfully in *Hard Times* by thinking of it in terms of monthly installments and by dividing it into three parts. This he did again in *A Tale of Two Cities,* but his approach to writing the novel was somewhat different this time.

To overcome the problem of his readers' receiving too small a portion at a time (Carlyle referred to these portions as teaspoonfuls), Dickens decided from the start to publish the novel simultaneously in weekly and monthly installments, with two illustrations in the monthly edition: "This will give *All the Year Round* always the interest and precedence of a fresh weekly portion during the month; and will give me my old standing with my old public, and the advantage (very necessary in this story) of having numbers of people who read it in no portions smaller than a monthly part" (Forster, 2:281). In his letters Dickens emphasized again and again the disadvantage of reading the story in weekly parts, or even monthly parts; he wanted his readers to see the whole design. And rightly so, for *A Tale of Two Cities* is very carefully plotted and brilliantly constructed.

Dickens considered the simultaneous publishing of weekly and monthly installments "a rather original and bold idea" (Forster, 2:280). But of more significance was the new approach Dickens was taking to the writing of the novel, as he explained in a letter to John Forster:

> Nothing but the interest of the subject, and the pleasure of striving with the difficulty of the form of treatment—nothing in the way of mere money, I mean—could else repay the time and trouble of the incessant condensation. But I set myself the little task of making *a picturesque story,* rising in every chapter, with characters true to nature, but whom the story should express more than they should express themselves by dialogue. I mean in other words, that I fancied a story of incident might be written (in place of the odious stuff that *is* written under that pretence), pounding the characters in its own mortar, and beating their interest out of them. If you could have read the story all at once, I hope you wouldn't have stopped half way. (Forster, 2:281)

A "story of incident" was very much a departure from the type of novel that Dickens's readers had come to expect. *Barnaby Rudge, Nicholas Nickleby, Martin Chuzzlewit, David Copperfield, Little Dorrit:* the titles of several of the novels alone indicate Dickens's emphasis on character. And the genius of his novels lies to a large extent in his dialogue, his keen ear for speech patterns and the revelation of character through language. Dickens's brilliance at re-creating his characters' speaking voices accounted for much of the success of his public readings. (He prepared a reading from *A Tale of Two Cities* entitled *The Bastille Prisoner,* but it was never performed.) Forster considered this new emphasis on incident and the revelation of character through action rather than through language a "hazardous" undertaking that "can hardly be called an entirely successful experiment" (Forster, 2:282). He criticized the depiction of character in the novel, but concluded that as "imaginative story-telling" it was "really remarkable" (Forster, 2:283). Forster underestimated the novel in many ways, but he was correct to praise its structure, in which "the domestic life of a few simple private people is in such a manner knitted and interwoven with the outbreak of a terrible public event, that the one seems but part of the other" (Forster, 2:283). Dickens too hoped that it was the "best story" (Nonesuch, 3:126) he had written, pointing out his emphasis on the plot; although the heroism of Sydney Carton is the raison d'être for the novel, the story line is the vehicle by which Carton's sacrifice gains its effect.

Small weekly units are in some ways an advantage in *A Tale of Two Cities* because they make possible several of the best effects in the novel. They allow, for example, the rapid switches from London to Paris, which draw attention both to the contrast between Soho and Saint Antoine and also to the ominous connection between them. We see in the chapter headings how often the short chapters are related either by contrast or by central idea: "A Sight," Darnay's trial, concludes in "A Disappointment"; "Monseigneur in Town" is followed by "Monseigneur in the Country"; "The Fellow of Delicacy," Stryver, is followed by "The Fellow of No Delicacy," Carton. "Knitting" is paired with "Still Knitting," and "One Night" with "Nine Days." "An Opinion" becomes "A Plea," and as book 2 reaches its fatal last chapter, "The Sea still rises" gives way to "Fire rises." In book 3, Carton's plan is put into motion in "A Hand at Cards" and "The Game Made," while "Dusk" becomes "Darkness." Most of these linked chapters occur together in one weekly part, and so form a complementary or contrasting unit, rising to a minor cliff-hanger at the end (more major suspense occurs at the end of each of the seven monthly parts). The Monseigneur chapters, for example, form a strong contrast between the indolent and artificial aristocrats of the Paris salon and the overtaxed, half-starved, and miserable peasants of the village, on whose backs the aristocrats have become fat and wealthy.

The linked chapters also move the story along swiftly, providing a strong sense of continuity and association within the story. This contiguity is perhaps the most striking aspect of the plot; the story marches to its grim conclusion as inexorably as the Revolution itself, the fruit of the "seed of rapacious license and oppression" (459).

The novel is shot through with repeated imagery and patterns of metaphor, the repetitions being too heavy-handed for some readers. We hear again and again the footsteps, the rising storm, the sound of the wild sea gathering force, the power of fire, and through it all the golden thread. But for the plot the main metaphor is the road, established at the end of the opening chapter when Dickens brings together the two countries, the two kings, the populace, and the characters in the novel as journeying "along the roads that lay before them" (4). The story really begins in the next chapter with the Dover road, which takes Mr. Lorry and, we hear later, also Lucie to Paris to bring back Doctor Manette. The headings of the three books emphasize this sense of a journey, of the story as a movement from one stage or state of being to another, held together by the central section, the "golden thread." Book 1, "Recalled to Life," is a transference from one spiritual state to another; book 3, "The Track of a Storm," is, we discover, a journey that leads to another such transference. There are many parallels between book 1 and book 3, which give the novel a satisfying sense of completion. Both books start with a journey to Paris—the first to release Doctor Manette, the second to release Gabelle—and in both Lucie is discovered to be traveling too. Both end with a hurried coach journey back to England, through the barriers requiring exit papers, with the coach containing Mr. Lorry, Lucie, and a "buried man who had been dug out" (58), in the first journey Doctor Manette, and in the second Charles Darnay.

Other roads memorably connect aspects of the plot. When the Marquis returns to his château, the mender of roads is a witness to a man hanging on underneath the coach; the man is of course Gaspard, whose child has been run over by that coach. When Gaspard kills the Marquis in revenge, he leaves a fitting note, "Drive him fast to his tomb" (154). The mender of roads reappears near the end of the novel, transformed into a wood sawyer and witness now to Lucie's daily visits to a street near the prison where she hopes Darnay may be able to see her from a window high in the prison wall. Just as the road mender's testimony led to Gaspard's arrest and execution, his testimony against Lucie would have been crucial in convicting her of plotting against the Republic.

The road to Paris, the road to the château, the streets of Saint Antoine on which the wine was spilled and Lucie paced, all give way to the streets along which the tumbrils "rumble, hollow and harsh" (459), taking Sydney Carton on his last journey as they have taken so many other victims, both guilty and innocent. Dickens merges the metaphor of the journey with that of sowing and reaping, one of the central metaphors of Carlyle's *French Revolution* (and also of *Hard Times*), when he says that the wheels of the tumbrils "seem to plough up a long crooked furrow among the populace in the streets. Ridges of faces are thrown to this side and to that, and the ploughs go steadily onward" (460). Inured to the spectacle, the people are ploughed through by the wheels of the death carts as relentlessly as Gaspard's little son was ploughed down by the Marquis's wheels.

After buying the drug that will allow him to smuggle Darnay out of the prison, Carton begins a night of wandering the streets of Paris (as Dickens himself frequently roamed city streets at night) with "the settled manner of a tired man, who had wandered and struggled and got lost, but who at length struck into his road and saw its end" (387). Carton's road leads him to the guillotine and a "violent passage into the other world" (69), as Dickens has satirically noted of the inn yard outside the Old Bailey. The poignancy of Carton's solitary journey to his death is heightened by its contrast with the flight of Darnay and the Manettes to England, which occurs at the same time. As the heavy tumbril rolls mechanically along, ploughing through the crowd and the mud alike, the coach taking the others to safety is hurrying through the French countryside, clattering over the stony ground, sticking in ruts, swerving in and out of the mud, "running—hiding—doing anything but stopping" (441). The jerky, breathless rhythms of the sentences describing the flight contrast very sharply with the mechanical, relentless prose that describes Carton's last journey: "Along the Paris streets, the death-carts rumble, hollow and harsh. Six tumbrils carry the day's wine to La Guillotine" (459).

The road at the opening of the novel that leads to these two last journeys is a favorite metaphor for the passage of life. Dickens used it in *David Copperfield*, when at the end of the novel David looks back over his life: "Long miles of road then opened out before my mind; and, toiling on, I saw a ragged way-worn boy, forsaken and neglected, who should come to call even the heart now beating against mine, his own."[1] The road gives *A Tale of Two Cities* a sense of direction, and at the novel's end it adds poignancy to the final vision of Carton as his road and that of the others, which had merged with the appearance of his riding cloak on the chair at Tellson's in Paris, are separated forever.

A Tale of Two Cities achieves its cohesiveness not just through repeated imagery but through the careful blending of the two plots, both in their impact on each other and in the gradual revelation of them. We have the surface happenings: Doctor Manette's return to England, Darnay's trial and marriage to Lucie, Gabelle's appeal for help, and Darnay's return to Paris. At each important scene in the story Carton appears, seemingly in a small role: as the offhand barrister at the Old Bailey trial, who casually provides the jury with the doubt that finds Darnay innocent; as the suitor of Lucie; and as an acquaintance in Paris. At the same time we have the continual presence of another plot, a hidden one, whose threads are revealed gradually until the final complete revelation at the reading of Doctor Manette's letter. In book 1 Mr. Lorry's troubled dreams in the fogbound coach raise questions about Doctor Manette's imprisonment: why was he imprisoned? who imprisoned him? In book 2 we see Doctor Manette gradually returning to his old clever self as a talented doctor, but with the shadow of the Bastille hanging over him still. Who is Charles Darnay, and why does his story about a buried letter in a cell in the Tower of London distress Manette so much? Why does he seem troubled by Darnay at first, and why does Darnay's revelation of his name (in secret to the Doctor on the morning of the wedding) strip Doctor Manette of his sanity and send him back to his imprisoned state of mind? Why does Darnay hate his uncle, and what was he really doing on the trips between France and England, which laid him open to the charge of treason? Whose footsteps are disturbing the quiet of Lucie's house in Soho? Does Defarge find anything in Manette's old cell in the Bastille? Why does Madame Defarge start when she hears that Lucie Manette has married Charles Evrémonde, alias Darnay? All of these questions are answered either in Doctor Manette's letter or by Madame Defarge after the final trial. But there is no trick ending here, no surprising overthrow of the reader's expectations, as happens in a detective novel, although Dickens creates suspense and suggests clues in the manner of the crime story (partly invented by his friend Wilkie Collins). Even Carton's sacrifice is only hinted at until Carton is actually in Darnay's cell.

We are gradually prepared for Doctor Manette's testimony through the questions we are led to ask as the surface story progresses. It is the method of all of Dickens's mature novels, a method described in *Great Expectations* through a haunting metaphor from Dickens's favorite book, the *Arabian Nights*. Pip is recounting how the reappearance of the convict, not seen or heard of since the opening chapters of the book but present throughout in small hints and clues,

overturns the solid foundation of Pip's life, just as the convict had
turned him upside down in the first chapter:

> In the Eastern story, the heavy slab that was to fall on the bed of
> state in the flush of conquest was slowly wrought out of the quarry,
> the tunnel for the rope to hold it in its place was slowly carried
> through the leagues of rock, the slab was slowly raised and fitted
> in the roof, the rope was rove to it and slowly taken through the
> miles of hollow to the great iron ring. All being made ready with
> much labour, and the hour come, the sultan was aroused in the dead
> of the night, and the sharpened axe that was to sever the rope from
> the great iron ring was put into his hand, and he struck with it, and
> the rope parted and rushed away, and the ceiling fell. So, in my case;
> all the work, near and afar, that tended to the end, had been accom-
> plished; and in an instant the blow was struck, and the roof of my
> stronghold dropped upon me.[2]

The roof of Darnay's stronghold drops as dramatically at the second French trial, and with as careful a preparation: the tying of Manette's troubled mind to Darnay himself, Defarge's searching of the
cell, Madame Defarge's pitiless involvement in the Terror—more relentless than that of any of the others except her counterpart, the Vengeance. Dickens deliberately keeps this subplot a mere suggestion,
hinted at very subtly in scenes such as Darnay's story of the prisoner
who hid a letter in his call. Manette brushes off his obvious distress at
hearing this story by referring to the coming storm: "There are large
drops of rain falling, and they made me start. We had better go in"
(119). From this hint of the hidden letter, Dickens makes the whole
scene a foreshadowing of the repercussions of the finding of Manette's
letter. Carton lounges in, and they group together at the window:

> Lucie sat by her father; Darnay sat beside her; Carton leaned
> against a window. The curtains were long and white, and some of
> the thunder-gusts that whirled into the corner, caught them up to
> the ceiling, and waved them like spectral wings.

"The rain-drops are still falling, large, heavy, and few," said Doctor Manette. "It comes slowly."

"It comes surely," said Carton.

They spoke low, as people watching and waiting mostly do; as people in a dark room, watching and waiting for Lightning, always do. (120)

Lightning is of course one of the metaphors for the Revolution, a part of "the Track of the Storm" that draws Darnay to Paris and Carton to the guillotine. We see it here for the first time, inextricably linked to the story of a hidden letter because it is the hidden letter that will bring about the final catastrophe. Lucie's footsteps are a further foreshadowing, as people below them in the street hurry for shelter and Lucie tells them how she imagines the echoes as "the footsteps of the people who are to come into my life, and my father's" (121).

Carton's place in the denouement after the reading of the hidden letter is foreshadowed at the end of this scene when he says of the footsteps coming into Lucie's life, "I take them into mine! . . . I ask no questions and make no stipulations. There is a great crowd bearing down upon us, Miss Manette, and I see them—by the Lightning. . . . And I hear them! . . . Here they come, fast, fierce, and furious!" (121–22) The hint given of the importance of a buried letter is thus given a dramatic intensity that both takes the reader's attention away from the hint itself and lays the ground metaphorically for the association of events that will arise from the discovery of that letter.

Dickens discusses his method in a letter to Wilkie Collins during the writing of the novel. Collins had apparently suggested that Doctor Manette reveal more about his background before the final revelation, but Dickens defends his method as being more natural:

I do not positively say that the point you put might not have been done in your manner; but I have a very strong conviction that it would have been overdone in that manner—too elaborately trapped, baited, and prepared—in the main anticipated, and its interest wasted. This is quite apart from the peculiarity of the Doctor's character, as affected by his imprisonment; which of itself would, to my thinking, render it quite out of the question to put the reader inside of him before the proper time, in respect of matters that were dim to himself through being, in a diseased way, morbidly shunned by him. I think the business of art is to lay all that ground carefully, not with the care that conceals itself—to show, by a backward light, what everything has been working to—but only to *suggest*, until the fulfilment comes. These are the ways of Providence, of which ways all art is but a little imitation. . . .

I am very glad you like it so much. It has greatly moved and excited me in the doing, and Heaven knows I have done my best and believed in it. (Nonesuch, 3:124–25)

That Dickens believed in his story, that he had "done and suffered it all" himself, is evident from the intensity of the emotions that we see in the coming storm, in the rising sea of revolutionaries, in the blood-stained stones of the Paris streets and the footsteps echoing in Soho Square. We know he thought of Sydney Carton while acting out Richard Wardour's death in *The Frozen Deep*, but is Carton the only hero of *A Tale of Two Cities?* And how did Dickens bring together the threads of his novel so cohesively? As usual, Dickens considered several titles for his novel before he hit on *A Tale of Two Cities*. Those other titles, though rejected, give us many clues to the central concerns of the novel and have an important bearing on how the themes and literary patterns of the novel were woven together so coherently.

8

"The Doctor of Beauvais"

Two of Dickens's proposed titles for *A Tale of Two Cities* would have centered attention on Doctor Manette: "The Doctor of Beauvais" and "Buried Alive." The public reading he prepared, but never gave, was also Manette's story, "The Bastille Prisoner." Without these signposts, the good doctor has been largely ignored in commentary on the novel, partly because the film versions that have popularized the book have made him seem old and rather pathetic. The harrowing picture of him as we first see him, with his wild tangle of white hair, his ragged beard and haggard face, becomes the impression viewers retain of him, and we tend to forget that he is only 45 when Mr. Lorry digs him out of his grave. In many ways the novel does revolve around Doctor Manette, and he plays a role very similar to hero, Sydney Carton eclipsing him only in the final few pages.

Doctor Manette is the heart of the novel from the start, occupying a central position in the plot that culminates in his testimony at the climax of the novel. It is Manette's story that begins the train of events 18 years before the opening of the novel. As the witness to the rape of a peasant girl and the murder of her brother by the Evrémonde brothers, he is witness to the class war that will result in the Revolution.

Just like the real Charles Dickens and Charles Father

68

"The Doctor of Beauvais"

Manette is French, but he belongs to neither class, being a middle-class doctor, a professional class that is otherwise lacking in Dickens's description of eighteenth-century France. The lawyers and merchants that Carlyle saw as playing a large role in the Revolution are nowhere to be seen either in Saint Antoine or at Monseigneur's salon. Doctor Manette is a man set apart right from the start, just as Carton will become set apart.

When we first hear of Manette he is a frightening prospect indeed. In the coach to Dover, Mr. Lorry has troubled waking dreams about his mission to bring back the Bastille prisoner who has been in a grave for 18 years: "After such imaginary discourse, the passenger in his fancy would dig, and dig, dig—now, with a spade, now with a great key, now with his hands—to dig this wretched creature out. Got out at last, with earth hanging about his face and hair, he would suddenly fall away to dust" (16). Lucie too is less than overjoyed at learning that the father she thought was dead has been found alive; it will be his ghost, she whispers, as though in a dream, not him. And in a sense he is a ghost at first, the empty shell of the man who was imprisoned 18 years before. He has forgotten even his name and is still held under lock and key because, as Defarge says, he is too inured to imprisonment to be able to bear freedom. (This was true of many released prisoners during the Revolution, who begged to be locked up again. Dickens makes the same observation in *Barnaby Rudge* when the prisoners released from Newgate are found lounging around its ruins the next day.)

The first sign that the ghost harbors in him the fragments of his earlier life is his recognition of Lucie, whom he mistakes for his wife. This transference of the past into the present through genealogy is played over again and again in the novel, both for good and for evil. We see it here as the first instance of the power of heredity to overcome even being buried alive. Dickens introduces one of his main themes at the beginning of chapter 3: "A wonderful fact to reflect upon, that every human creature is constituted to be that profound secret and mystery to every other" (12). Even the closeness of father and daughter cannot completely overcome this secrecy. When Darnay asks Doctor Manette if Lucie thinks favorably of him, Manette answers, "My daughter Lucie is, in this one respect, such a mystery to me; I can make no guess at the state of her heart" (162). Dickens plays upon this secrecy throughout the novel, but in heredity we see one way that this mystery is overcome. Doctor Manette is a stranger to Lucie, but her resemblance to her mother is the tie that brings him back from the grave of his mental imprisonment. Gradually, under her care, he becomes again the man her mother knew.

It is the power of heredity that consoles Sydney Carton as he goes to his death also, thinking of Lucie's children, one of them named for him and making that name illustrious again. There is even a grandson in the picture, also named for Carton, who will visit the site of the guillotine when the Terror is long past.

Heredity is also a source of evil, however. Because he is an Evrémonde, Darnay is sentenced to death for the sins of his fathers. Nothing he can do in his own right can save him from his lineage, and Madame Defarge is ready to extend the sentence to his wife and their child as well, because they too are Evrémondes. It is the ancient curse that underlies the concept of original sin, that all children are born with the sins of Adam and Eve on their heads. It pervaded Greek thought also, and in Madame Defarge's relentless pursuit of the family that destroyed her family we see the Greek insistence that murder be avenged by the relatives of the victims, regardless of circumstances.

Doctor Manette continues to be a dual personality, half Lucie's father, restored to active life, half her mother's husband, the ghostly dug-up remains of an 18-year burial. This duality is particularly striking at the Old Bailey trial, where the spectators see in him "a certain indescribable intensity of face: not of an active kind, but pondering and self-communing. When this expression was upon him, he looked as if he were old; but when it was stirred and broken up—as it was now, in a moment, on his speaking to his daughter—he became a handsome man, not past the prime of life" (73).

Doctor Manette's lapses into the person he was in the Bastille tie the immediate action of the novel to the subplot: the rape of the peasant girl and the murder of her brother; Darnay's attempts to fulfill his mother's wishes for atonement; Madame Defarge's attempts to gain revenge on the Evrémondes; and finally the reading of Manette's hidden letter. That the lapses are beyond the doctor's control is made clear by his conversation with Mr. Lorry after the revelation of Darnay's real name brings on a nine-day relapse into his Bastille state. Manette confesses to Mr. Lorry that he feels the lapses coming on and fights against them, but cannot prevent them from happening if something triggers the old remembrances. It is clear, however, that Doctor Manette does recall the source of his suffering and suspects that Darnay is associated with the Evrémondes even before his name is revealed on the wedding morning. When Darnay declares his love for Lucie, Manette says to him, "If there were . . . any fancies, any reasons, any apprehensions, anything whatsoever, new or old, against the man she really loved—the direct responsibility thereof not lying on his head—they should all be obliterated for her sake. She is everything to me; more to me than suffering, more to me than wrong, more to me—Well! This is idle talk" (162–63). The depth of Manette's character is revealed here, as he not only prepares to give up to another man the one woman on earth he loves, but also resolves to bury the cause of his 18 years of suffering. Manette is willing to sacrifice his own happiness for Darnay, for Lucie has made it clear that she would stay unmarried with her father if he desired it. His reason for refusing her offer—that her life would be "wasted . . . struck aside from the natural order of things," (227)—shows Manette's sanity in a world characterized by the perversion of the natural.

Manette buries his knowledge of Darnay's ancestry and its connection with his own life at great cost. Even in sleep, Manette struggles to keep his knowledge of the terrible injustices done to him a secret: "Into his handsome face, the bitter waters of captivity had worn; but, he covered up their tracks with a determination so strong, that he held the mastery of them even in his sleep. A more remarkable face in its quiet, resolute, and guarded struggle with an unseen assailant, was not to be beheld in all the wide dominions of sleep, that night" (231). Manette is the embodiment of the Christian tenet of forgiveness, in opposition to Madame Defarge, whose desire to avenge past wrongs is halted only by her death. In Doctor Manette can be seen the roots of Miss Havisham in *Great Expectations,* the crazed woman who has locked herself away ever since her fiancé jilted her on her wedding day. With the clocks stopped at the time when she heard the news of his betrayal, Miss Havisham is "buried alive" in a tomb of her own making, her wedding dress decaying on her, the rats nibbling at the cobweb-covered wedding cake on the table. Doctor Manette returns to the Bastille years only sporadically, when something triggers a mental relapse, but when that relapse occurs he is tied to the occupations and circumstances that caused his initial suffering. He seems to be able to overcome it when Lucie needs his help after Darnay's arrest: "And when Jarvis Lorry saw the kindled eyes, the resolute face, the calm strong look and bearing of the man whose life always seemed to him to have been stopped, like a clock, for so many years, and then set going again with an energy which had lain dormant during the cessation of its usefulness, he believed" (333). Miss Havisham is never released from her prison; vowing revenge, like Madame Defarge, she turns her latent energy into a self-destructive vendetta against all men and uses Estella, her only source of love, as a weapon of hate. Doctor Manette is able to use his lifeline Lucie as a source of health and freedom from the past, turning his energies outside himself to the care of others.

Part of Manette's success in overcoming the shadow of the Bastille is this energy, a characteristic that Dickens also possessed. It is evident even when he sleeps; it is his recipe for recovering from his lapses into the past, as he explains to Mr. Lorry: "It may be the character of his mind, to be always in singular need of occupation. That may be, in part, natural to it; in part, the result of affliction. The less it was occupied with healthy things, the more it would be in danger of turning in the unhealthy direction" (246). Just as Dickens makes fun of Wilkie Collins's indolence as Thomas Idle in comparison to his own energy as Frances Goodchild in *The Lazy Tour of Two Idle Apprentices,* in all his novels he attributes the Victorian virtues of earnestness, activity, and exertion to the heroes, in contrast to the apathy and indifference of their rivals. Often apathy is seen to be a facade, a fashionable pose adopted by young men, usually in answer to their father's desire that they do something useful. Eugene Wrayburn is such a poseur in *Our Mutual Friend,* but he is forced to drop the facade at last when he is saved from drowning by the intensely active and courageous heroine. In Carton too we see a man who has accepted his apathetic role and resigned himself to a passive, wasted life.

Doctor Manette quickly returns to the vitality that characterized him before his arrest, a vitality that sets him apart in book 3. He discovers that his imprisonment is the source of his newfound strength; he has been reborn with even greater energy than before: "For the first time the Doctor felt, now, that his suffering was strength and power. For the first time he felt that in that sharp fire, he had slowly forged the iron which could break the prison door of his daughter's husband, and deliver him" (333). In the literary tradition of the journey to the underworld, undertaken by Odysseus in the *Odyssey* and by Christian heroes in the valley of the shadow of death, the hero returns from his brush with death a wiser and stronger person. Manette's strength is philosophically the result of his 18 years of being buried alive and practically the result of being a Bastille prisoner and thus a hero to the Revolutionaries. He is a man set apart, able to walk through the Terror as though he were indeed a ghost:

> Still, the Doctor walked among the terrors with a steady head. No man better known than he, in Paris at that day; no man in a stranger situation. Silent, humane, indispensable in hospital and prison, using his art equally among assassins and victims, he was a man apart. In the exercise of his skill, the appearance and the story of the Bastille Captive removed him from all other men. He was not suspected or brought in question, any more than if he had indeed been recalled to life some eighteen years before, or were a Spirit moving among mortals. (337)

Manette is set apart, not just as a hero of the Revolution, but as an impartial doctor, "using his art equally among assassins and victims." As a doctor, his "business was with all degrees of mankind, bond and free, rich and poor, bad and good" (333–34), an ideal that lay at the heart of *A Christmas Carol,* one of Dickens's most powerful social criticisms. In that book, the character Scrooge prides himself on being a man of business and tells the charity gentlemen that the poor are not his business: "It's enough for a man to understand his own business, and not to interfere with other people's" (*CB,* 12). When he is visited by the ghost of his old partner, Marley, who laments his wasted life, Scrooge reminds him that he was "always a good man of business, Jacob." But Marley replies: "Business! . . . Mankind was my business. The common welfare was my business; charity, mercy, forebearance, and benevolence, were all my business. The dealings of my trade were but a drop of water in the comprehensive ocean of my business!" (*CB,* 21–22).

The difference between economic business and moral business is seen clearly in Mr. Lorry, who thinks he exemplifies Tellson's Scrooge-like emphasis on business rather than emotions, but who gradually reveals the virtues of Marley's human business. But Doctor Manette demonstrates most clearly this quality of universal compassion. The ancien régime, represented by the Evrémonde brothers, shares Scrooge's view that the poor have nothing to do with them and that they have no responsibility toward them (and Dickens emphasizes how great that responsibility really was; the villagers fear that Gaspard may be cruelly tortured because in killing the Monseigneur he was killing his father, as the Monseigneur is considered the father of his tenants). Unfortunately once the Revolution takes hold, the sansculottes are equally callous about their "business" and will sacrifice anyone for the good of an institution, the Republic.

Doctor Manette saves Darnay at the first French trial and feels the same sense of jubilation that he has saved Darnay for his beloved Lucie as Carton feels at the third rescue of Darnay, when he takes his place on the scaffold. The parallels between Doctor Manette and Carton draw closer together as the book nears its end and Carton takes Manette's place as the center of the action. Both men are inspired by Lucie and are prepared to risk anything to keep the man she loves beside her. Both have a wasted and spiritually dead past that has a grip over their present actions that they are unable to shake off. But both find that past the source of their strength when the time comes to use it. When Manette's power in the land is taken away by his own testimony against Darnay, Carton steps in and takes over the doctor's role. As Darnay is led out the prisoners' door, Lucie faints at her father's feet: "Then, issuing from the obscure corner from which he had never moved, Sydney Carton came and took her up" (414). He does so with an air "that had a flush of pride in it," just as Manette "was proud of his strength" (354) when he saves Darnay from the first tribunal.

Doctor Manette is a worthy hero and a crucial piece in the puzzle. His energy is shown to be the opposite of the fierce energy of the Revolution: he is a victim of the ancien régime just as surely as Madame Defarge is, even more so, but the smoldering fire lit by his imprisonment bursts into a flame of humanitarian work that is seen in opposition to the thirst for revenge that has taken over the oppressed peasants at the grindstone. As they mow down innocent and guilty alike, Doctor Manette moves calmly through them, tending to everyone equally as human beings, not as members of any class. That his protection of Darnay and his family is eventually taken away by Madame Defarge, reducing him once again to his mindless state, indicates how the Revolution eventually turns on the revolutionaries; as Carlyle says, "The Revolution, then, is verily devouring its own children? All Anarchy, by the nature of it, is not only destructive but *self-destructive*" (*FR*, 2:383). Doctor Manette is immune from harm at first because he is considered a friend to the Jacquerie, having been a victim of the aristocracy. Ernest Defarge would continue to give him a victim's protection and extend it to his daughter and granddaughter, but Madame Defarge, like the hungry guillotine itself, would have them all exterminated. It was characteristic of the Revolution that the heroes one day were the enemy the next; one by one the leaders were turned upon and sent to the guillotine themselves, as were Madame Defarge and the rest of the Jacquerie.

In suggesting the title "The Doctor of Beauvais" Dickens was acknowledging Doctor Manette's heroic role in the novel, his central position in the whole of the first part, and his isolated and active role in the third. His sacrifices, while not as dramatic as Carton's, are still noble. As Darnay acknowledges after the trial, Doctor Manette silently overcame his bitter hatred of Darnay's family for Lucie's sake, struggling in secret with his "natural antipathy" (413) against Darnay, at great cost to his own mental health. After the first French trial, when Manette does save Darnay from death, he was "recompensed for his suffering" (354) and "happy in the return he had made" Lucie. Darnay acknowledges his father-in-law's actions when he says, "No other man in all this France could have done what he has done for me" (353). Manette's actions in book 3 prepare for the rise of Sydney Carton to take his place as hero when the old doctor succumbs once again to his mental illness. Carton is also recompensed for the suffering he undergoes when he is turned down by Lucie. He too saves her husband out of a sense of indebtedness to her because she understood his secret heart and was sympathetic to him. Dickens has hinted at the way Carton will replace Manette as Lucie's protector and Darnay's saviour in the earlier English scenes. After Mr. Lorry and Miss Pross "murder" Doctor Manette's shoemaker's bench in the hopes of murdering also the hold his imprisonment retains over his mind, the next chapter opens with Carton's appearance in Soho Square with the request that he and Darnay be friends. He asks that he be allowed to visit freely and be regarded "as an useless . . . an unornamental, piece of furniture, tolerated for its old service, and taken no notice of" (253). Carton seems quite clearly to be replacing the old, unornamental but serviceable shoemaker's bench, the prop upon which Doctor Manette relies when he loses his hold on the present. Thus when his next relapse occurs, after the reading of his letter at Darnay's trial, it is Carton who steps in and makes the Doctor's recovery possible by saving his daughter and her husband.

While Doctor Manette would willingly have given his life for Lucie's happiness at the end of the book, such a sacrifice would have been undramatic. An old man now, and unbalanced, who could weep at his death if it saved his daughter and her family? He has been an exemplary hero throughout, returning from the grave, braving the wild mob of the Revolution alone and unscathed, providing the climactic evidence in court. But Maria Ternan (Ellen's sister) did not weep over the body of a white-haired grandfather; she wept over Richard Wardour. And so the novel becomes Sydney Carton's after all.

9

"Memory Carton"

When in 1855 Dickens began his *Book of Memoranda* with ideas for his writing, the germ of Sydney Carton was his second entry: "The drunken?—dissipated?—what?—LION—and his JACKALL and Primer—stealing down to him at unwonted hours" (*Memoranda*, 1). In a long list of possible names for characters a few pages later, the names Carton and Striver-Stryver appear, and Carton is suggested as the title for a book that would be "a story in two periods—with a lapse of time between, like a French Drama" (*Memoranda*, 5). Most of the titles have to do with time, as does "Memory Carton," and many of them contain echoes of *A Tale of Two Cities* and its insistent reminder of the passage of individual human time in the larger context of historical time: "Two Generations," "Rolling Years," "Day after Day," "Many Years' Leaves." Dickens used the name Carton in his 1857 Christmas book *The Perils of Certain English Prisoners;* it was a good solid English name for a good solid English officer. But what did he mean by Memory Carton, and how did this title find a home in *A Tale of Two Cities?*

Dickens had been looking for a new, unconventional hero when he brought his influence to bear on Wilkie Collins's *The Frozen Deep* and devised the character of Richard Wardour. Up to that time his heroes had been morally upright and admirable, and above all likeable, even the half-wit Barnaby Rudge or the indecisive Arthur Clennam of *Little Dorrit,* the novel that preceded *A Tale of Two Cities.* But Dickens was tiring of the stereotype and hankered after a hero who could rise to that stature from less promising beginnings, whose story would be the victory of a better, inner self over the callous, worldly one that had grown up over the years. He had devised such a character in the five Christmas books, written between 1843 and 1848, but these were short moral tales. In a letter to John Forster in August 1856, he wrote of his frustration at having to produce conventional heroes:

> I have always a fine feeling of the honest state into which we have got, when some smooth gentleman says to me or to someone else when I am by, how odd it is that the hero of an English book is always uninteresting—too good—not natural, etc. I am continually hearing this of Scott from English people here [in France], who pass their lives with Balzac and Sand. But O my smooth friend, what a shining impostor you must think yourself and what an ass you must think me, when you suppose that by putting a brazen face upon it you can blot out of my knowledge the fact that this same unnatural young gentleman (if to be decent is to be necessarily unnatural), whom you meet in those other books and in mine, *must* be presented to you in that unnatural aspect by reason of your morality, and is not to have, I will not say any of the indecencies you like, but not even any of the experiences, trials, perplexities, and confusions inseparable from the making or unmaking of all men! (Forster, 2:267)

Richard Wardour has been a thoroughly unlikable man, gruff, rude, jealous, disdainful of other people. Although in asides he has revealed a better nature crushed by the disappointment of his rejection by the woman he loved, it is only at the end that he overcomes his bitter, resentful feelings to sacrifice his own life for the life of his rival. On the page Richard Wardour does not rise above the third-rate play in which he appears; only Dickens's acting could give him any sort of stature. But Sydney Carton, while inspired by Wardour, has captivated readers and achieved a following shared by very few of Dickens's more conventional heroes.

From the start Carton is a mysterious figure, partly because of Dickens's intention that the characters should be expressed through the story rather than through dialogue, and partly because of the role he plays in the novel. When we first see him he is silently contemplating the ceiling while Darnay fights for his life in the dock of the Old Bailey. The courtroom is divided into two vocal factions: the witnesses for the prosecution and the spectators who, buzzing like flies and supported by the attorney general, eagerly await a guilty verdict; and Lucie and her father, anxiously testifying on the prisoner's behalf but innocently harming his case at the same time. Carton is unattached, seemingly uninterested, yet holds the key to the case; tossing a crumpled ball of paper toward his senior, the lawyer for the defense, Carton points out the weakness in the prosecution's argument and saves Darnay's life.

Carton's place in this scene typifies the place he occupies in the rest of the novel: a bystander, caught between the crowd (later the Paris mob) and the Manette/Darnay family. As he stares at the ceiling he seems oblivious of the proceedings and unconcerned that a man's fate is hanging in the balance. His manner, "so careless as to be almost insolent" (90), masks a deep concern for how the proceedings affect Lucie, as Dickens reveals when Carton is the first to notice that she is nearly fainting. This seeming obliviousness that hides an acute perception of the truth is Carton's main trait throughout the novel.

From the start Carton has typified Dickens's observation that "every human creature is constituted to be that profound secret and mystery to every other" (12). Barsad finds Sydney Carton a mystery when the "hand at cards" is played out and Carton blackmails Barsad into helping with Darnay's rescue, and in many ways Dickens keeps Carton a mystery to the reader as well. The reasons for Carton's morose disregard for life and inability to make anything of his career are never really stated, but he suffers from the disease of apathy that affects many of Dickens's later heroes. His failure to throw off this apathy, become the "lion" rather than the "jackal," is more convincing than Dickens's portrayal of him as a wastrel and a drunkard, the unconventional hero that Dickens defended in his August 1856 letter to Forster. We see little that would convince us that Carton is really a profligate, but there is truth in Dickens's view of him as a solitary man whose inner goodness has somehow failed to shine: "the cloud of caring for nothing, which over-shadowed him with such a fatal darkness, was very rarely pierced by the light within him" (179). There are parallels here with Doctor Manette, for Manette too has been overshadowed with the fatal darkness of the Bastille, but the light within him breaks out and disperses the gloom most of the time. He tells Lucie that if he had prevented her from marrying "the dark part of my life would have cast its shadow beyond myself, and would have fallen on you" (228). Whereas there seems to be no reason for Carton's "fatal darkness," Manette's reason is all too clear and understandable.

Carton's past remains in shadow. There are no secret revelations, long buried, to tell us why he became the man he did. We learn that his mother had died when he was young and that when "he had been famous among his earliest competitors as a youth of great promise" (387), his father had died also. This lack of background is unusual for a Dickensian hero, most of whom have complicated pasts that are slowly revealed, as Manette's and Darnay's are, by the unfolding of the plot. But this lack is purposeful on Dickens's part, given the role that Carton plays in the novel. He is a man set apart, with no connection to the French Revolution or to the Manette/Evrémonde/Defarge story until he forges a connection himself at the end. His moral lassitude does not even seem to be the result of the social times, as outlined in the opening chapter, except, perhaps, as a comment on the futility of the legal system. If justice is meted out as arbitrarily as it is shown to be at the Old Bailey trial, why should a barrister take any real interest in it? Like Carton's dealings with Barsad at the end of the novel, it is merely a game.

Carton, in his solitary and purposeless wanderings through the London streets, stands apart from the main action as he seemed apart from the trial at the Old Bailey. But he is drawn to the Manette family through his love for Lucie, and this love inspires his altered attitude to life in the third part, when he can throw off the shadow of his past apathy and become active for her sake, like Doctor Manette. But whereas Manette acts in a public sphere, ministering to the wounded and taking part in the happenings, Carton remains a private figure. Even his arrival in Paris is mysterious, his presence announced through his clothing: "Who could that be with Mr. Lorry—the owner of the riding-coat upon the chair—who must not be seen?" (345). When Carton's inner light begins to shine through his habitual malaise, the nature of his private self becomes more clearly visible against the secret selves of the other characters. Manette is crippled by his secret life, the knowledge of his suffering that is fully revealed at the reading of the letter and results in his collapse into a senseless Bastille prisoner again. Jerry Cruncher's secret life as a "resurrection man," who digs up bodies to be sold to surgeons for research, is fully revealed to Mr. Lorry at the end when Lorry expresses his horror that Cruncher has been using Tellson's as a respectable front for his illegal secret occupation. Immediately after Jerry's revelation, Carton reveals his true nature to Mr. Lorry, and at the same time Mr. Lorry drops his business exterior and reveals his own soft heart to Carton.

On the night before his execution, Carton goes through the valley of the shadow and comes out strong enough to make the final sacrifice and redeem his wasted life. This redemption is anticipated early in the novel when, after an all-night drinking bout with Stryver, Carton walks home through the chilly, deserted, early-morning streets of London. The setting, "like a lifeless desert," is an expression of his own spiritual lassitude, but just as London will come to life with the rising of the sun and the activities of the day, Carton too has the potential for rebirth: "Waste forces within him, and a desert all around, this man stood still on his way across a silent terrace, and saw for a moment, lying in the wilderness before him, a mirage of honourable ambition, self-denial, and perseverance. In the fair city of this vision, there were airy galleries from which the loves and graces looked upon him, gardens in which the fruits of life hung ripening, waters of Hope that sparkled in his sight. A moment, and it was gone" (106). The vision of a transformed city and a redeemed life can be only a vision at this point, but it shows Carton's potential. His vision of the "fair city" will be borne out in his final prophecy of "a beautiful city and a brilliant people rising from this abyss" (465) to reveal Dickens's hope that through individual spiritual redemption, society too will cast off the evils of cruelty and inhumanity.

Carton walks the streets of Paris, not aimlessly as he had walked in London, but with "the settled manner of a tired man, who had wandered and struggled and got lost, but who at length struck into his road and saw its end" (387). The passage takes place at night; Carton crosses the Seine, as travelers to the other kingdom in Greek mythology cross the river Styx, and carries a child across a muddy street. For a few moments the world stands still, "as if Creation were delivered over to Death's dominion" (389), but with the rising of the sun Carton falls asleep, his journey through the valley of the shadow complete, and he awakes to his last day with the courage of the old heroes. Psychologically his death and rebirth have already occurred.

Why did Dickens consider calling the novel "Memory Carton," and why does Stryver call Carton "Memory"? The place of memory in the human psyche is a central concern in all Dickens's works, particularly the ones that succeeded the Christmas books. The first step in Scrooge's conversion from a miserable miser to an open-hearted, loving man is taken when he is forced to remember what he was as a child. For Dickens the memory of our childhood innocence and spontaneity is the key to unlock the prisons of the mind that make adults repressed, selfish, and self-absorbed. The hero of the fifth Christmas book, *The Haunted Man,* is taught by his double that without the memory of suffering and wrong we can have no compassion, no artistic sensibility, no humanity. It is memory that keeps alive the imaginative side of our natures.

Memory is presented more ambiguously in *A Tale of Two Cities.* Dickens had written *The Haunted Man* in the earnest hope of convincing himself that his own unhappy memories were beneficial rather than crippling. But in Doctor Manette we see how the memory of his Bastille days spells mental disaster for him; when the memories are aroused too forcefully, as in Darnay's story of the hidden letter in the Tower, and the knowledge of Darnay's real name, Manette reverts hopelessly to that past and is powerless to prevent his loss of reason. When he writes down his sufferings with the express purpose of not allowing them to be forgotten, he innocently writes Darnay's sentence of death. Madame Defarge too is an implacable enemy because she lives in the memory of her sister's rape and her brother's murder. She cannot see the present for what it is, just as Manette cannot voluntarily hold on to his present mental health. In *A Tale of Two Cities*, memory, far from allowing the person an imaginative and softening return to a childlike innocence, actually imprisons the mind and prevents it from reacting vitally in the present.

"Memory Carton." In many ways the title is misleading, as spoken by the ever-ironic Stryver about his drunken jackal. Carton seldom seems to look back into the past; he is crippled not by regrets but by inertia and a lack of faith in himself. It is memory, however, inspired by Lucie, that eventually brings about the change of direction in him, as he admits to her in his revelation of his love for her: "the sight of you with your father ... has stirred old shadows that I thought had died out of me. Since I knew you, I have been troubled by a remorse that I thought would never reproach me again, and have heard whispers from old voices impelling me upward, that I thought were silent for ever. I have had unformed ideas of striving afresh, beginning anew, shaking off sloth and sensuality, and fighting out the abandoned fight" (182). The language is melodramatic, but Carton seems to believe that he has, until meeting Lucie, lacked the influence of parents, the "old voices" that guided his childhood. Darnay also listens to the voices from his past; his desire to right the wrongs of his family is primarily due to his mother's reliance on him to do so.

Carton tells Lucie that he will carry the remembrance that he opened his heart to her through the rest of his "misdirected life" (182), and Lucie too carries his secret within her. It underlies his final sacrifice, when he kisses Lucie for the last time and her child later recalls that she heard him say, "a life you love" (415), the words Carton had used when he told Lucie that he would "give his life, to keep a life you love beside you!" (184). The scene is recalled again when Carton has Darnay write to Lucie in words that are clearly Carton's and are intended to remind her of their earlier conversation.

Carton's final act is thus partly inspired by memory, the knowledge that he opened his heart to Lucie and admitted that he had a better self. But the final sacrifice is imbued not with the past but with the future. As Carton goes to the scaffold he thinks not of what might have been but of what is to come. He sees his own future in the reiterated words, "I am the Resurrection and the Life, saith the Lord: he that believeth in me, though he were dead, yet shall he live: and whosoever liveth and believeth in me shall never die" (464). And he sees the future of his friends and enemies, and France itself, foreshadowed in the prophetic vision that fulfills his earlier mirage in the streets of London. This vision allows him to see himself, not just resurrected to a new heavenly life, but working out a new earthly life through Lucie's ancestors who will bear his name. When Carton dies with the words "It is a far, far better thing that I do, than I have ever done," he is renouncing the mental prison that has prevented him from making something of his life; he is living dynamically, as Doctor Manette does, and even if for him the action is soon over, its repercussions will be felt for as long as the Darnay family survives.

10

"Buried Alive"

When Dickens suggested "Buried Alive" as a possible title for his new novel, he asked John Forster if it seemed "too grim?" (Forster, 2: 280). Grim indeed, and it is little wonder that Dickens rejected that title in favor of *A Tale of Two Cities*. But it was a fitting title too, for "buried alive" is the major theme of the novel, from Doctor Manette's recall to life to Charles Darnay's repeated recall from the edge of the grave. Carton tells Lucie that he is "like one who died young" (181). "Buried alive" runs as a ghostly and sometimes chilling refrain, recurring in different forms in both the public and private events, and in physical and psychological forms. But it has a positive side too, in the recurring symbol of resurrection and rebirth.

When Dickens proposed "Buried Alive" as his title he was thinking primarily of Doctor Manette's recall to life. We have seen how as early as 1846 he was considering a story about "a man imprisoned for ten or fifteen years," an idea prompted perhaps by his discussions with a prison doctor in Lausanne that year. Dickens's fascination with prisons, both as a fact of nineteenth-century life and as a metaphor for mental states, was lifelong, beginning with his father's imprisonment in the Marshalsea Prison for debt. Because of his father's imprison-

86

ment, Dickens was mentally and physically "buried alive" in the grim and dirty blacking factory, mindlessly pasting labels on bottles when he should have been at school. The Marshalsea dominates *Little Dorrit*, the novel that preceded *A Tale of Two Cities*, and Newgate prison, in which Darnay is incarcerated before his trial for treason, is the focus of *Great Expectations*. When Pip first sees Newgate its grim gray bulk is nearly blocking out the spiritual center of London, Saint Paul's. In *Barnaby Rudge*, Newgate is attacked and burned by the rioters in a scene that prefigures the storming of the Bastille in *A Tale of Two Cities*.

Prisons dominate *A Tale of Two Cities* also, symbols of the oppression of the ancien régime that incarcerated innocent victims like Manette in the Bastille, and of the oppression of the revolutionaries, who similarly imprisoned any apparent enemy of the Republic without due process of law. Dickens had contemporary accounts to draw upon for his portrayal of the prison system in Revolutionary Paris, but he also drew upon his own extensive knowledge of prisons from his boyhood visits to his father in the Marshalsea and from later visits to prisons in England and America. Of particular relevance for *A Tale of Two Cities* was his 1842 visit to the famous Cherry Hill Penitentiary in Philadelphia, an "international showplace for the Separate System,"[1] which he was criticized for condemning in *American Notes*. Most English prisons of the time followed the Silent System, which allowed prisoners to work and eat together but without communicating by word or even sign. Under the separate system prisoners were kept in solitary confinement for the whole of their incarceration, which was often many years, the argument being that association with other prisoners prevented reformation. Certainly many successful crimes were planned in prison, and the silent system was introduced to try and overcome this problem also, but the advocates of the separate system claimed for their method that living with only one's conscience and religious and moral texts was the best road to reform.

Dickens was appalled by what he saw in the Philadelphia prison and wrote about it movingly in *American Notes* and in letters to John Forster:

I went last Tuesday to the Eastern Penitentiary near Philadelphia, which is the only prison in the States, or I believe, in the world, on the principle of hopeless, strict, and unrelaxed solitary confinement, during the whole term of the sentence. It is wonderfully kept, but a most dreadful, fearful place. . . . Every prisoner who comes into the jail, comes at night; is put into a bath, and dressed in the prison garb; and then a black hood is drawn over his face and head, and he is led to the cell from which he never stirs again until his whole period of confinement has expired. I looked at some of them with the same awe as I should have looked at men who had been buried alive, and dug up again. (Forster, 1:211–12)

Dickens told Forster that he later argued with the prison inspectors about the system, for, he wrote, "although the inspectors are extremely kind and benevolent men, I question whether they are sufficiently acquainted with the human mind to know what it is they are doing" (Forster, 1:212).

Dickens mulled over the impression of men "buried alive" from 1842 to 1859, when in Doctor Manette he could show what solitary confinement might do to the human mind. He was prepared to admit that for short sentences the separate system might have the reforming effect that its proponents believed it did, and certainly after 10 years Doctor Manette is still capable of penning the long history of his unjust imprisonment. But Dickens reviled the system very forcefully for its long-term harm in *American Notes:*

I believe that very few men are capable of estimating the immense amount of torture and agony which this dreadful punishment, prolonged for years, inflicts upon the sufferers; and in guessing at it myself, and in reasoning from what I have seen written upon their faces, and what to my certain knowledge they feel within, I am only the more convinced that there is a depth of terrible endurance in it which none but the sufferers themselves can fathom, and which no man has a right to inflict upon his fellow-creature. I hold this slow and daily tampering with the mysteries of the brain, to be immeasurably worse than any torture of the body: and because its ghastly signs and tokens are not so palpable to the eye and sense of touch

as scars upon the flesh; because its wounds are not upon the surface, and it extorts few cries that human ears can hear; therefore I
the more denounce it, as a secret punishment which slumbering humanity is not roused up to stay.[2]

The depth of suffering hidden in the "mysteries of the brain" is forcibly presented in Doctor Manette's lapses into his prison state of mind,
lapses that can occur years after his release.

Dickens's description of the Bastille brings vividly to the reader's
mind the impression of being "buried alive." As Defarge and Jacques
Three make their way through the prison to Manette's old cell, they
leave behind the crowd besieging the outside walls and find themselves
alone, "hemmed in here by the massive thickness of walls and arches."
Their senses, and thus their links with the outside world, are gradually
stifled, as the tumult outside comes to them "in a dull, subdued way,
as if the noise out of which they had come had almost destroyed their
sense of hearing." The passageways had never seen the light of day,
and even in Manette's cell "the sky could be only seen by stooping low
and looking up" (266). The cell, with its blackened walls, deep in the
inner tower of the Bastille, is a grave indeed.

Charles Darnay is threatened with the fate of being "buried alive"
when his fellow prisoners at La Force lament that he is to be "in secret," in solitary confinement. The parallels with Manette's imprisonment in the Bastille are made clear when Darnay asks, "I am not to
be buried there, prejudged, and without any means of presenting my
case?" (309) In using the phrase "buried alive" to describe Darnay,
Manette, and the Philadelphia prisoners, Dickens is drawing attention
to the inhumanity of separating people from the lifeblood of the human condition, communication with others. Without such society, the
mind becomes crippled and loses touch with reality, as Dickens demonstrates in his 1861 Christmas story, *Tom Tiddler's Ground*, which
castigates a hermit for his misanthropic solitude and shows how a
small girl when left alone falls into self-pity and general bad temper.

"In secret" in this context reveals a different way of looking at
Dickens's earlier reflection "that every human creature is constituted

to be that profound secret and mystery to every other" (12). Dickens asserts here that every heart is "in some of its imaginings, a secret to the heart nearest it." We see this secrecy in Lucie's knowledge of Carton that she does not pass on to Darnay, the "heart nearest" hers. We see it in Manette's constant struggle to keep the secret of his suffering from those around him, the struggle surfacing on his face. The small secrecies of the heart, only "some of its imaginings," are thus contrasted with the enforced total secrecy of the thoughts of the prisoner in solitary confinement and are seen to be the healthy mysteries of the human mind as opposed to the harmful torments of the prisoner who cannot communicate his thoughts. Manette seeks such communication when he writes his long letter, hoping ironically that "some pitying hand" (394) may find it long after he is dead, a voice from the grave. The need for human contact is made very clear at the end when Carton and the little seamstress, strangers and therefore as unknown to each other as the bundled-up travelers in the coach to Dover, find strength through their mutual recognition of each other's quiet heroism. Their short but vital journey together confirms the need for human contact; although they know nothing about each other, their hearts recognize the value of true Christian compassion, shared "in secret" by two people against the inhuman throng watching them. Their thoughts, buried alive in them, are allowed to surface and sustain them.

"Buried alive" is the predicament of Manette and the Philadelphia prisoners, living men in gravelike cells. But "buried alive" has other connotations, which are worked out in A Tale of Two Cities to reveal the perversion of the natural world that the Revolution engendered. Burial of the dead is one of the most sacred of religious rituals, regardless of the religion and the customs practiced. Of the many rites of passage in human affairs, the passage from this world to the next is the most mysterious and solemn, requiring in most cultures a ritualized practice to ensure that the journey is properly undertaken. The ancient Greeks, for example, buried their dead with a coin under their tongue, to pay the ferryman Charon and ensure their passage to the next world. To pretend to be dead, to stage a mock funeral and burial and then to be "reborn" under another name and identity as old Foulon and Roger Cly do in the novel is thus a travesty of an important rite, the sacrilegious use of a sacred ritual for their own ends.

But more horrifyingly sacrilegious are the activities of the "resurrection man," Jerry Cruncher, who digs up corpses from their graves and sells them to surgeons for anatomy experiments. It was a lucrative underground profession that came to the attention of an unknowing public when in 1828 William Burke and his accomplice Hare were revealed to have murdered at least 16 people in order to sell their bodies to an Edinburgh surgeon. Their story is told in "Use and Abuse of the Dead," an article by Dickens's colleague Henry Morley, which appeared in *Household Words* on 3 April 1858. Morley also reports on the London partnership of Bishop and Williams, who claimed to have sold from 500 to a 1,000 bodies over a 12-year period and who confessed to three murders. Like Burke, Bishop and Williams were hanged and ended up in the dissection room themselves. The grisly details of the activities of these resurrection men led to the passing of the Anatomy Act in 1832, which provided that bodies must be made available for medical dissection.

The whole notion of "resurrection men," of removing bodies from their final resting place and selling them for gain, runs through the novel as a chilling antithesis to the Christian meaning of resurrection: man's rebirth after death into eternal life through the power of Christ. This sacred resurrection surrounds Carton's last hours, of course, as his mind reiterates Christ's assurance of everlasting life. Carton not only finds consolation in the words; he becomes a Christ figure himself, sacrificing his own life for the life of Lucie and her family. Innocent of any wrong, he is put to death that others may live.

Jerry Cruncher has Christ's initials and, in his macabre second profession as an "honest tradesman," carries on, under cover of darkness, a removal of bodies that mocks the discovery of Christ's empty grave after the Crucifixion. Even in his legitimate employment Jerry is connected with rites of passage, as he watches the streams of humanity flowing down Fleet Street twice a day, "both ever tending to the plains beyond the range of red and purple where the sun goes down!" (185). But Jerry is described here as being like "the heathen rustic," the observer of a pagan rite rather than a Christian one. Everything about Jerry reveals a perversion of the Christian themes underlying the novel. His brutal treatment of his wife, who is guilty only of the sin of praying for him, is a perversion of the Christian marriage vows and is witnessed by their son. Young Jerry also witnesses his father's criminal grave robbing and is terrified by it; in opposition to the loving fathers in the novel—Gaspard, Darnay, and Manette—Jerry provides a counterpoint, sometimes comic, sometimes frightening. He even echoes Carton's rebirth into a better life at the end when he assures Mr. Lorry that he will give up grave robbing and take up "flopping," or praying, like his wife. Jerry's change of heart is perhaps a pity at this point, however, as it tends to undercut the nobility of Carton's sacrifice.[3] Dickens intentionally brought Madame Defarge to an ignoble death to make Carton's end more heroic, but such a contrast is lost in Jerry Cruncher's transformation. Jerry is even allowed to share in Carton's rescue of Darnay, as his knowledge of Cly's fake burial allows Carton to blackmail John Barsad and gain access to Darnay's cell.

"Buried alive" thus can be the destructive incarceration of men and women in solitary cells like 105 North Tower, or the burying of secret selves, a past life hidden in the psyche but waiting to surface, for good or evil. But the novel's final affirmation of the positive aspects of being "buried alive" asserts the concept of Christian resurrection, that when the body is buried the soul is "buried alive," ready for rebirth. Some critics have complained that Dickens's Christian vision here is shown to be insincere because of his reference to Carton and the little seamstress as "these two children of the Universal Mother" (463). But Dickens here is calling attention to his overlying themes that human affairs are a part of the natural world and that the horrors of the Revolution were a perversion of the natural, turning men into monsters as surely as the ancien régime had also perverted the natural order. Christ's resurrection is the Christian version of a process of the natural world that finds expression in all religions. In order to grow again in the spring the flowers in the garden must be buried alive, lying apparently dead but actually only dormant, waiting for the warmth of spring to bring them to life again. Dickens mulled over this idea and how it relates to people as well as to plants in his *Book of Memoranda* in 1855:

> "There is some virtue in him too."
>
> "Virtue! Yes. So there is in any grain of seed in a seedsman's shop—but you must put it in the ground, before you can get any good out of it."
>
> "Do you mean that *he* must be put in the ground before any good comes of *him?*"
>
> "Indeed I do. You may call it burying him, or you may call it sowing him, as you like. You must set him in the earth, before you get any good of him." (*Memoranda*, 4)

Most people are allowed their dark night of the soul, their setting in the earth, without actually losing their life. Scrooge thinks he has had to forfeit his life when he is shown his gravestone, but he rejoices to find that the ghosts have managed his conversion in a single night, and he awakens on Christmas Day feeling "quite a baby" (*CB*, 85). In *Great Expectations* Pip, though nearly killed by Orlick in the lime kiln, lives to repent his poor treatment of Joe. But Sydney Carton's final words reveal that his capacity for doing a "better thing" can be fulfilled only by his death. For Carton, "you must set him in the earth, before you get any good of him."

11

"The Thread of Gold": Women and Marriage

When Dickens suggested "The Thread of Gold" for the title of the novel, he was intending it to be Lucie Manette's story. And in many ways it is. The Bastille prisoner is recalled to life through her agency; Darnay's new life is bound up with hers; Carton is inspired to his supreme sacrifice because of his love for her and his recognition of her goodness. She is central to the actions of nearly all the characters except perhaps the Crunchers: Mr. Lorry is devoted to her and acts throughout the novel largely out of this devotion; Miss Pross too is governed in her actions solely by her love of Lucie. Madame Defarge directs her anger against Lucie because she is Darnay's wife and because she therefore represents the aristocratic wife whose death will somehow compensate for the sufferings of the peasant wives and children. In many ways the characters are also paired around the central figure of Lucie. Miss Pross is pitted against Madame Defarge, and their final fatal meeting is caused by Miss Pross's attempts to prevent Madame Defarge from finding Lucie and condemning her to the tribunal. Carton and Darnay, physical doubles, are rivals for Lucie's love. Stryver and Carton both aspire to her hand, but Carton's unselfish love for her is contrasted with Stryver's selfish desire to own a wife as he would a piece of property. Darnay and Manette love her enough to share her because, as Darnay tells her, she is able to spare enough of herself to keep everyone happy.

We have seen how Lucie's characterization derived from Dickens's childhood friend Lucy Stroughill, his golden-haired neighbor, and the golden-haired Lucy from *The Wreck of the Golden Mary* who, like Lucie Manette, is the inspiration that keeps hope alive in the desperate survivors of the shipwreck. "Lucie" means light, and both characters take on a religious significance as the possessors of a spiritual purity. The golden thread too has religious connotations. It is traditionally a metaphor for the inviolable heart of things, the sacred core of truth and honesty that binds together the more vulnerable pieces of the fabric. In English law it refers to the tenet that a man is innocent until he is proven guilty. Without the golden thread, any other virtues in the system cannot survive. And so it is with Lucie, who gives meaning and purpose to the lives of Darnay, Carton, Manette, Miss Pross, and Mr. Lorry. There are many connecting threads in the book, such as Manette's connection to Darnay and the Defarges, but whereas these threads lead to the revelation of hidden sufferings and repressed guilt, Lucie's golden thread binds the characters into an indestructible web of love that will prove stronger than Madame Defarge's powerful lust for revenge.

Lucie's golden thread is contrasted throughout the novel with the wool that Madame Defarge silently and purposefully knits into her register, condemning those named in her pattern to the guillotine. Darnay's name is there; so is Lucie's. If Lucie represents the golden thread, the pure heart of love, truth, and justice, Madame Defarge represents fate, but fate in the hands of man rather than God and therefore flawed and unjust. Here again we can see parallels with classical literature, where taking fate into your own hands always results in tragedy. Oedipus thought he could outwit his fate by moving away from his father's house, but his actions led him to meet his fate and kill his father instead. Shakespeare, too, frequently demonstrated the difference between providence, or God's will, and the foolish man's belief that fate is arbitrary or can be controlled by man. In *Hamlet*, for ex-

ample, the wise characters like Horatio put their trust in God's providence, as Hamlet does at the end, whereas the foolish characters like
Polonius and Rosencrantz and Guildenstern believe in Fate and come
to arbitrary and undignified ends, killed by mistake in place of someone else. Such is Madame Defarge's end, killed by the accidental firing
of her gun when she is attempting to bring about Lucie's death. Like
Hamlet, Madame Defarge makes the mistake of thinking she can avenge a relative's death by taking the law into her own hands and dealing out her own justice against her persecutors. Hamlet is driven by
his father's ghost to try to kill Claudius, but he eventually comes to
realize that "there's a divinity that shapes our ends, / Rough-hew them
how we will" (5.2.10–11). He puts his faith in divine providence, as
Horatio had advised from the start when he tells the guards that
"Heaven will direct it" (1.4.91). Gaspard too suffers because he per-
sonally punishes the Marquis for killing his son. Carton's final faith
that divine justice will prevail is derived from Lucie's strong faith that
gives her the courage to endure the trials of her position as Manette's
daughter and Darnay's wife.

Lucie has been criticized as being a faceless character, too good
to be true and lacking in dimension. Certainly her speech is often lu-
dicrously stagy, as in her first long address to her father when the
refrain "weep for it" (54) merely adds to the sentimentality of her
words. Her conversation with Carton is equally melodramatic. But we
have already seen how Dickens intended the characters to be "true to
nature, but whom the story should express more than they should
express themselves by dialogue" (Forster, 2:281). Seen through her
actions, Lucie is anything but a melodramatic stage heroine; rather,
she is a courageous woman like the British women caught in the
bloodbath of the Indian Massacre whom Dickens wanted to honor in
The Perils of Certain English Prisoners. Heroic women took an increasingly major role in Dickens's later novels, perhaps through the
influence of Ellen Ternan. Ellen had played the part of another heroic
Lucy, Lucy Crayford in *The Frozen Deep*, and Dickens certainly was
thinking of her when he named Estella in *Great Expectations* and Helena Landless in *Edwin Drood* (Ellen's middle name was Lawless). Lu-

cie's bravery is the determined but patient courage that Dickens talked of as "quiet heroism" in *The Battle of Life*. Like Little Dorrit in the novel preceding *A Tale of Two Cities*, Lucie is the sole support of an imprisoned and sometimes mentally deranged father. Although she fears the footsteps that seem to be threatening Soho and dreads the shadow that Madame Defarge casts over her, she is resilient enough to brave the dangerous streets of Paris to stand beneath the prison wall every day, in the hopes that Darnay may see her there. The thread of gold that binds her to him would lead her, as Carton tells Mr. Lorry, to "lay her own fair head beside her husband's cheerfully" (426) on the guillotine. Lucie's role in the book is to provide the moral center from which the people surrounding her draw their strength. She is less active than the later heroines of *Our Mutual Friend* and *Edwin Drood,* Lizzie Hexam and Helena Landless, because that sort of tough, aggressive woman is seen in Miss Pross and taken to horrifying extremes in Madame Defarge. Lizzie Hexam rescues Eugene Wrayburn (a dissolute waster like Carton) from drowning because she is a skillful oarswoman and is able to pull him to safety. Because Madame Defarge and Miss Pross share this physical strength, Lucie's strength is mental and emotional, but she exemplifies the qualities of a genuine hero: strength, dedication, patience, and bravery.

Lucie's golden thread of calm and rationality is seen as the antithesis of the mad turbulence of the Revolution, just as her devotion to her family reveals how far the revolutionary women have been driven from their natural roles as wives and mothers. Lucie and the little seamstress, busy with the traditional occupations of womanhood that benefit those around them, are contrasted with the "knitting women" whose "fingers . . . were vicious, with the experience that they could tear" (270). The women's fingers tear at old Foulon, who "told my baby it might suck grass, when these breasts were dry with want!" (273). The cruelties of the ancien régime that deprived these women of the ability to fulfill their most basic instinct, the need to feed their children, "laid a dreadfully disfiguring hand" (447) upon them.

At the same time the aristocratic women whose husbands frequented the Monseigneur's salon have rejected this same basic instinct.

"Except for the mere act of bringing a troublesome creature into this world" (126), these women have nothing to do with their children, preferring to turn the task of mothering them over to peasant women. Dickens suggests that these country women, who "kept the unfashionable babies close, and brought them up," have thus been archetypal mothers, nurturing not only their own children but the neglected children of rich women too immature to raise them themselves. That the suffering of their children has turned these peasant mothers into wild beasts, "with streaming hair, urging one another, and themselves, to madness with the wildest cries and actions" (272) is all the more tragic.

Just as Dickens uses Jerry Cruncher's grave-robbing and later reformation as a counterpoint to Carton's Christ-like sacrifice, so he sets different types of marriage against each other in the book and by doing so demonstrates his range of understanding of domestic relationships. Dickens is frequently criticized for his depiction of the Victorian ideal of the hearth and home with a dutiful wife, submissive and devotedly subordinate to her husband. Lucie is certainly dutiful and devoted to Charles Darnay, but he is dutiful and devoted to her also; as husband and wife they are mutually loving and equally respected. That a submissive wife is not a healthy attribute of an ideal marriage is made clear when Stryver and Carton discuss Stryver's plans to marry. Stryver's attitude typifies the views of many Victorian men when he urged Carton to find "some respectable woman with a little property" who will "take care of you" (169). By marrying Lucie, Stryver looks forward to having a "home when he feels inclined to go to it (when he doesn't, he can stay away)," and a wife who "will always do me credit" (169). Stryver's view of a wife as an appendage of the man with no life of her own, useful only in what she can do for her husband, is shown to be as utterly despicable as the man himself.[1]

The Crunchers offer a further counterpoint to the stereotype of the submissive wife. Jerry's attacks on his wife, both physical and mental, are brought on because he believes she is not conforming to the standards of the dutiful wife and mother. He accuses her of praying against him when he finds her on her knees and berates her for interfering with "the profit of the business" (195). Mrs. Cruncher is understandably appalled by her husband's illegal and irreligious trade in dead bodies, but Jerry turns her concern against her in his efforts to convince himself that he is an "honest tradesman" conducting a business like any other. He berates her for not fulfilling the Christian duties of a wife and mother, accusing her of starving their son by preventing Jerry from making money, and of failing to "honour and obey" (195) as the Christian marriage service dictated. Like Stryver, he considers women intellectually inferior to men, worthy only to act as servants to their masters: " 'It's enough for you,' retorted Mr. Cruncher, 'to be the wife of an honest tradesman, and not to occupy your female mind with calculations when he took to his trade or when he didn't. A honouring and obeying wife would let his trade alone altogether. Call yourself a religious woman? If you're a religious woman, give me a irreligious one! You have no more nat'ral sense of duty than the bed of this here Thames river has of a pile, and similarly it must be knocked into you' " (196). Young Jerry witnesses his father's attack on his mother as Jerry takes her by the ears on the bed and knocks her head against the headboard. He has just witnessed his father's "fishing" also, and although he is terrified by what he sees, the next morning he tells Jerry that he wants to be a resurrection man when he grows up. We can presume that he will also adopt his father's brutal treatment of women.

The Cruncher scenes are usually regarded as the comic interludes in this least comic of Dickens's novels. But Jerry's abuse of his wife is far from comic and is condemned as roundly as Stryver's similar attitudes. The difference between them is a class one: Stryver talks of retreating to his club when he feels like it and of his raising Lucie up to his station, where she will "tell well" (169). Cruncher, a working man, has similar ideas about his wife's duties to him, but without the resources of male clubs and the money to enjoy them he comes home and beats her. Mrs. Cruncher is a gentle, honest woman who assures her husband that her prayers "only come from the heart, Jerry. They are worth no more than that" (63). Jerry's attitudes to marriage parallel his attitudes to his illegal work: in both Jerry desecrates Christian tenets, while turning his desecration into a virtue. As the "honest tradesman" he is simply trying to provide food for his child; his wife's opposition to it proves that it is she who is at fault in the marriage.

A comic parallel to the Crunchers is Miss Pross and her brother, Solomon, alias John Barsad. Solomon, like Jerry, lives a double life, but his criminal activities as a spy are not known to his trusting sister, whose gullibility knows no bounds when it comes to admiring her good-for-nothing brother. When they meet unexpectedly in Paris, Miss Pross comes in for exactly the same criticism that Jerry had leveled at his wife. Solomon accuses his sister of wanting to see him caught and punished for being a spy, "Just as I am getting on!" (365), he complains. Like Jerry, he considers his underground occupation a worthy business that his interfering sister would put a stop to. Like Mrs. Cruncher, Miss Pross takes the blame for their estrangement on her own shoulders, while Solomon treats her with "far more grudging condescension and patronage than he could have shown if their relative merits and positions had been reversed" (365–66). Once again it is the woman who is honest, decent, and compassionate, the man who is leading an illegal double life and pretending a moral superiority to the woman he has robbed.

At the center of the book are the Defarges, and here the stereotype of the submissive wife is completely turned on its head in the portrait of Thérèse, in all ways the dominant force in the marriage. When Defarge is downhearted at the slowness of the progress toward the Revolution, Thérèse's defiant and animal-like patience shames him into attempting to echo her determination. He stands "before her with his head a little bent, and his hands clasped at his back, like a docile and attentive pupil before his catechist" (216). As so often in the novel, a religious image is used to demonstrate the perversion of religious ideals. But Defarge's uncertainty becomes increasingly a virtue as his wife becomes increasingly inhuman. "Let loose a tiger and a devil" (217), she declares in this scene, and that is exactly what she becomes when she stalks Lucie and her daughter. Defarge tries to save Lucie and Doctor Manette from Thérèse's condemnation, but he has no power against his wife and is totally dominated by her. His greater humanity is no match for her will, just as Barsad is no match for her greater cunning and intelligence.

Besides the loving partnership of Charles and Lucie, one other couple makes a brief appearance to exemplify an ideal marriage. As the Marquis's coach makes its way to the château, it passes a wayside shrine where a woman is praying. She stops the coach and entreats the Marquis to provide a simple marker for her husband's grave, which lies under "a little heap of poor grass" and will soon be forgotten, as he and the countless other peasants who have died of want are forgotten. The Marquis thinks at first that she wants him to overlook a debt of her husband's, because for a man like the Marquis human relations have been reduced to purely monetary transactions. When she replies that he has "paid all . . . he is dead," the Marquis asks sarcastically, echoing the resurrection theme, "Can I restore him to you?" The Marquis's valet puts her away from the coach, and the Marquis hurries on, but the reader is left with an indelible impression of the widow's humanity and suffering: "She looked an old woman, but was young. Her manner was one of passionate grief; by turns she clasped her veinous and knotted hands together with wild energy, and laid one of them on the carriage-door—tenderly, caressingly, as if it had been a human breast, and could be expected to feel the appealing touch" (139). In this brief encounter Dickens encapsulates for us the situation of the novel and acts out Madame Defarge's sister's grief as well. A victim of the Marquis's lack of compassion, the widow asks only that her husband be buried properly. The woman's work-worn hand is yet a gentle and caring hand, one that has not yet been formed into the vicious fingers of the knitters who wish to tear Foulon to pieces.

Three other women remind us that women have an important part to play in the novel. The little seamstress exemplifies a peasant woman who has not been disfigured by the times, and she acts as a parallel to Lucie, providing a loving heart for Carton when Lucie's is retreating from Paris with Darnay. Similarly Darnay's mother exemplifies an aristocrat who has not been corrupted by wealth and power. Although the Marquis's wife does not make a physical appearance in the novel, she dominates it quite subtly from the beginning. It is her pity for the Defarge family, and her outrage at her husband's treatment of them that governs Charles Darnay's actions throughout the book, as he tries to "execute the last request of my dear mother's lips, and obey the last look of my dear mother's eyes, which implored me to have mercy and to redress" (147–48). Her compassion, like Doctor Manette's and Lucie's, cuts across all lines of class and privilege. Like Lucie's golden thread, it offers an example to Darnay and causes him, not just to reject his aristocratic background, but actively to try and redress the wrongs that his family has perpetrated.

Finally, the heroic Sydney Carton is compared as he approaches the guillotine to "one of the most remarkable sufferers by the same axe—a woman" (464). She was Madame Roland, whose noble death is described sympathetically by Carlyle. "Queenly, sublime in her un-complaining sorrow" (FR, 2:338), she walked to the guillotine with a man called Lamarche "whose dejection she endeavored to cheer," just as Carton helps to sustain the little seamstress. Madame Roland's request for pen and paper, that she might write down her thoughts, was refused, and she uttered instead the now well-known phrase to the Statue of Liberty, which stood by the scaffold: "O Liberty, what things are done in thy name!" (FR, 2:339–40). To show Lamarche how easy it was to die she asked to be guillotined first, and so went to her death with "as brave a heart as ever beat in woman's bosom!"

That Dickens recalls Madame Roland's bravery to his readers as Carton performs his final heroic deed is significant of the primary role women play in the novel. He makes a woman, Madame Defarge, the leader of his revolutionaries because for Dickens the cruelty of the women was the most unnatural aspect of a revolution that he saw as the overturning of natural, human decency and goodness. Being a woman, she epitomizes for him the worst excesses of the transforma-tion of people into wild animals, because he sees women as possessing the greatest claim to compassion and humanity. Madame Defarge's ruthless bravery in her cause is contrasted with the heroism of her victims. Whether it is the devoted bravery of Miss Pross, the long-suffering and patient fortitude of Mrs. Cruncher, or the compassion-ate, loving courage of Lucie and her golden thread, it is women who provide the essential core of humanity and decency in those disjointed times.

12

Shadows and Seas:
Patterns of Imagery

Some readers of *A Tale of Two Cities* feel swamped—even drowned—
by the intensity of the imagery that pervades the book. We have already seen how the historical scenes like the storming of the Bastille
are awash in images of a raging sea. But Dickens does not stop here:
footsteps follow, echoes reverberate, shadows fall, and storms,
whether at sea or on land, crash and thunder and din about our ears
seemingly without cease. It is an extremely noisy novel. But it was an
extremely noisy revolution also, and Dickens places his story in the
reverberations of shadow, storm, fire, and water with great control
and for well-defined thematic reasons.

The thread of gold emphasizes the wholeness of life, the connections between people that struck Dickens so forcefully. He repeatedly
defended his novels against the charge that the plots relied too much
upon coincidence by pointing out how frequently the paths of our lives
do cross and recross and how often odd coincidences occur in real life.
In *A Tale of Two Cities* he was particularly concerned with the way
in which lives overlap, impinge on each other, and influence future
lives through the individual's place in historical time. In the mass
movement of the French Revolution, which later observers tend to see

as a clash of one class against another, overlooking the individual, Dickens was concerned to show how the upheaval in society threw the connection between individuals into relief and forced the juxtaposition of unlikely people in unlikely places. Like Oedipus on his ill-fated road to Thebes, thinking he is leaving his father behind but actually walking toward his kingdom, many of the characters are drawn to the Loadstone Rock of Paris as surely as Darnay is because of the interconnectedness of their pasts and futures.

To create this sense of lives overlapping and past events determining later ones, Dickens casts shadows over the novel from the opening; in chapter 3, "The Night Shadows," he introduces in brilliantly descriptive terms the twofold intention of shadows in the story. These shadows are both "outside the coach" (16), in the swirling mists that surround the plodding horses on the muddy hill, and inside Mr. Lorry's head as he hallucinates about digging up Doctor Manette. These internal psychological shadows that arise from Manette's imprisonment will be felt again and again throughout the novel.

The external shadows conceal Jerry Cruncher, who is bringing a message to Mr. Lorry but is mistaken by the guards and their passengers for a highwayman. The guards, Tom and Joe, have something in common with the men on the battlements at the opening of *Hamlet,* fearful of the figure looming out of the mist and puzzled by the exchange between the figure and the person it has come to address:

> "What did you make of it, Tom?"
> "Nothing at all Joe."
> "That's a coincidence, too," the guard mused, "for I made the same of it myself." (11)

Dickens surely had *Hamlet* in mind in the Shooter's Hill descriptions, for in both play and novel the opening scenes of guards in the dark confronting an unknown and fearful visitor establish the situation of the plot. In *Hamlet* the visitor is of course the ghost of Hamlet's father; in *A Tale of Two Cities* the visitor is Jerry with news relating to Doctor Manette, who in the nightmares that trouble Jarvis Lorry is very definitely a ghost also. When Lucie is first told about Manette in the next chapter, she also is "going to see his Ghost! It will be his Ghost—not him!" (29). Both eerie scenes tell us that there is trouble in the land. In *Hamlet* the guards on the battlements of Elsinore are "sick at heart" (1:1:8), sensing an as yet unknown corruption in the land. "Something is rotten in the state of Denmark" (1:4:90), warns Marcellus later, just before the ghost of the dead king reveals to Hamlet that the new king, Claudius, is a usurper and murderer and consequently has thrown the kingdom into an unnatural state. As Hamlet exclaims, "The time is out of joint" (1:5:189). The Dover coach guards are not affected by the coming revolution (although the novel's beginning hints that England should be fearful too), but Doctor Manette's ghost, who troubles Mr. Lorry, is, like Hamlet's ghost, going to demand that its persecutors be punished. Just as Hamlet's father asks Hamlet to avenge his murder by killing Claudius, Doctor Manette, through his buried letter, will denounce the Evrémondes and their descendants and invoke in the tribunal's audience "the most revengeful passions of the time" (410). Dickens even uses Shakespeare's metaphor when he refers to the dancers in the Carmagnole as "types of the disjointed time" (343).

The shadows that pervade Shooter's Hill also suggest that the reality hidden behind them is dark and threatening, like a violent highwayman or the hidden story behind a Bastille prisoner. The night shadows that Manette's resurrection have thrown over Mr. Lorry's mind recur in different forms and remind us that the past will eventually enter the present. The Bastille shadow clings to Manette when he emerges from the Old Bailey after Darnay's acquittal, and the changes that come over his face involuntarily then are "as incomprehensible to those unacquainted with his story as if they had seen the shadow of the actual Bastille thrown upon him by a summer sun, when the substance was three hundred miles away" (92). In the very next scene Manette comes face to face with Darnay for the first time and immediately recognizes something familiar and fearful about him (his resemblance, of course, to his father and uncle). Manette's face "had become frozen, as it were, in a very curious look at Darnay: an intent look, depending into a frown of dislike and distrust, not even unmixed with fear," but he "slowly shook the shadow off" (94) and turned to Lucie. The use of "shadow" here associates Darnay with the shadow of the Bastille that has fallen over Manette and that will fall over Darnay in turn when its substance is revealed at the reading of Manette's letter. The shadows of the Bastille fall over Manette involuntarily, but they become triggered with increasing frequency by Darnay's presence.

Bound up in Manette's shadow of the Bastille is the shadow of poor Gaspard's hanged body, which "struck across the church, across the mill, across the prison—seemed to strike across the earth, messieurs, to where the sky rests upon it!" (207). Gaspard, like Manette, is a victim of the Marquis's cruelty, and here the violence of the class war that killed Gaspard's child, the Marquis, and Gaspard himself will have implications for every aspect of French society and for the greater cosmos.

The shadow haunting Manette recurs most threateningly in that which Madame Defarge casts over Lucie, and this shadow is also caused by the Evrémondes. In the chapter "The Shadow" Lucie is first made aware of the threat that Madame Defarge embodies. Like the footsteps in Soho, the shadow is formless but pervasive, and it troubles the perceptive Lucie even while Mr. Lorry, always trying to be "businesslike," assures her, "A shadow indeed! No substance in it, Lucie" (330).

Both shadows—that of Manette when it troubled Mr. Lorry in the coach and showed in Manette's face, and that of Madame Defarge when she silently tracked Lucie as her prey—are brought into the light with the reading of Manette's denunciation in the chapter "The Substance of the Shadow." Here the full import of the night shadows both inside and outside the coach is revealed, and the complex connections between Manette, the Evrémondes, and the Defarges reach their tragic climax. Shadows, with all their implications of darkness, fear, and foreboding, are shown to be horrifyingly substantial.[1]

The images of deluge and storm, lightning, earthquake, and flood that give the novel a sweeping sense of cataclysmic change are elemental; they enforce Dickens's view of the Revolution as a descent into hell that can be redeemed by Christian resurrection. The descent is marked by archetypal figures who exist in a kind of primordial state. The book opens 14 years before the storming of the Bastille when

> rooted in the woods of France and Norway, there were growing trees, when that sufferer was put to death, already marked by the Woodman, Fate, to come down and be sawn into boards, to make a certain movable framework with a sack and a knife in it, terrible in history. It is likely enough that in the rough outhouses of some tillers of the heavy lands adjacent to Paris, there were sheltered from the weather that very day, rude carts, bespattered with rustic mire, snuffed about by pigs, and roosted in by poultry, which the Farmer, Death, had already set apart to be his tumbrils of the Revolution. But that Woodman and that Farmer, though they work unceasingly, work silently, and no one heard them as they went about with muffled tread. (2–3)

Similar to these rustic workers is the mythical creature who sets fire to the country châteaux, "a shaggy-haired man, of almost barbarian aspect, tall, in wooden shoes that were clumsy even to the eyes of a mender of roads, grim, rough, swart, steeped in the mud and dust of many highways, dank with the marshy moisture of many low grounds, sprinkled with the thorns and leaves and moss of many byways through woods" (278). This strange man, seeming to be more beast than human, suddenly appears before the mender of roads as though he has emerged from some antediluvian mud. His "benighted mind" can comprehend only the most elemental act, reducing the ostentatiously civilized châteaux of the privileged to ashes. His deadly work creates "a red-hot wind, driving straight from the infernal regions" (283).

These elemental images form the religious framework of the novel by tying together Christian belief and the natural cycle of death and rebirth. The novel abounds with biblical references, but the most striking are those connected with water, wine, and blood. The spilt cask of wine in the first French scene is a brilliant depiction of the transformation of water into wine, and wine into blood. As the gutters flow with wine rather than rain the starving peasants frantically lap it up as it streams through the cobble stones. (Dickens had described such a scene before in *Barnaby Rudge,* when the rioters set fire to a vintner's house and drink themselves to death as the spirits pour down the street.) Then in a grim foreshadowing of the blood that is soon to flow over those same cobblestones, Gaspard writes the word BLOOD in wine on the wall. The reference of course is to the Christian sacrament of Holy Communion, which re-creates Christ's invitation to his disciples at the Last Supper to drink the wine in the cup because it is his blood, shed for mankind. The crazed drinking of the wine among the cobbles becomes the even more crazed violence of the Terror as the wine stains become blood stains, but in the final reenactment of Christ's sacrifice, Sydney Carton's blood is shed that another may live. Death has been turned into life.

The transubstantiation is reversed for Madame Defarge, whose feet are met by water from a broken basin when she confronts Miss Pross and her own imminent death. The peasants who drank the spilled wine at the beginning "had acquired a tigerish smear about the mouth" (34), a smear transformed by the Terror into the grim figure of Madame Defarge, whom "opportunity had developed ... into a tigress" (447). Madame Defarge is figuratively swept away by the water that had swirled in a maelstrom around her wine shop, the victim of her own violence. And in that washing away of Madame Defarge Paris is purged of one of its most vicious citizens.

The many references to water, especially torrential, apocalyptic water in the form of wild seas and storms and lashing rain, tie the Revolution into the theme of the novel by suggesting rebirth and renewal. Described so often as a terrifying reversal of the natural order in which people are turned into beasts, the Revolution is shown through the images of water to be a disaster that will yet result in the washing away of wrong and the rebirth of a better order of society. The coming of rain, always associated with renewal and baptism, is movingly described in the Soho scene when Darnay's story of the

Tower has just awakened Doctor Manette's memories of his own buried letter. Manette attributes his look of terror to the large drops of rain that have fallen on his hand, obliquely linking his history of suffering with the coming Revolution. The link is made evident when, the rain continuing to fall, Doctor Manette comments, "It comes slowly," to which Carton replies, with a clear reference to the Revolution, "It comes surely" (120). The rush of footsteps outside adds to the connection between Soho and France, as the watchers continue to use ambiguous pronouns that refer both to raindrops and to the marshaling of revolutionaries in Saint Antoine:

> "And I hear them!" he added again, after a peal of thunder. "Here they come, fast, fierce, and furious!"
> It was the rush and roar of rain that he typified, and it stopped him, for no voice could be heard in it. A memorable storm of thunder and lightning broke with that sweep of water, and there was not a moment's interval in crash, and fire, and rain, until after the moon rose at midnight. (122)

Dickens repeatedly casts the human action in the elemental terms of flood, rain, seas, and storm because he wants to emphasize that the enormity of the Revolution's destruction will result in the washing away of the old evils, and the rebirth of a new order. Such is Carton's vision as he steps up to the scaffold: "I see a beautiful city and a brilliant people rising from this abyss, and, in their struggles to be truly free, in their triumphs and defeats, through long long years to come, I see the evil of this time and of the previous time of which this is the natural birth, gradually making expiation for itself and wearing out" (465).

Birth and rebirth are always painful and difficult; the bringing about of new life or a new order requires the often violent overthrow of the old. But in tying the history of a people to the natural phenomena of sea and storm (the real sea at Dover was equally destructive when Mr. Lorry was waiting to sail to France), Dickens reminds us that despite the pain a new and better order will emerge. Carton's death is a kind of drowning also, a baptism that results in his resurrection into a "better rest." (Again there are echoes of Hamlet, whose dying words are "The rest is silence" [5.2.368].) As Carton takes his last steps, "the murmuring of many voices, the upturning of many faces, the pressing on of many footsteps in the outskirts of the crowd, so that it swells forward in a mass, like one great heave of water, all flashes away. Twenty-Three" (464).

13

"A Tale of Two Cities"

On 11 March 1859 Dickens could report to his friend John Forster that he had at last hit on the perfect title for his new story, "exactly what will fit the opening to a T. A TALE OF TWO CITIES" (Forster, 2:280). It was certainly the right title for the opening passages that describe France and England through a series of comparisons. But from the antitheses of that famous opening, "It was the best of times, it was the worst of times," to the balanced parallelism of Carton's final lines, "It is a far, far better thing I do, than I have ever done; it is a far, far better rest I go to than I have ever known," the new title also fitted to a T Dickens's use of doublings in the style and content of the novel. Twofold structures based on both contrasts and parallels reinforce a novel based on two cities, two countries, and two heroes who look the same. Through these doublings Dickens reinforces the twofold nature of his vision of the French Revolution and its aftermath: the passage from humanity to bestiality that marked the ancien régime as well as the Terror, but then the movement from darkness to light, and from destruction to rebirth.

We have seen how the plot depends on contrasting scenes, especially the contrasting of Lucie's peaceful and secure home in Soho with the inhuman "homes" of the Marquis in the Parisian salon and in his stony château, and with the Defarges' equally barren wine shop. The decadence of the aristocrats in the salon is contrasted with the poverty of the village people clustered round the fountain at the Marquis's country home. His cruelty in both places is linked by the fountain image: Gaspard's child is killed beside the Paris fountain, and Gaspard's hanged body poisons the village fountain and therefore the lives of the villagers.[1] The water that should bring life now brings death, and the starving peasants who have no bread create a guillotine with an insatiable appetite for blood. The two trials of Darnay are compared, for in both he is tried for acts against the state, Manette is a witness against him, and he is "recalled to life" by the action of Carton. In both trials the public is eager for a conviction, and the prosecution seems to care little about the due process of law. But whereas in the English court justice does prevail in the end, the French court demonstrates the impossibility of any justice or mercy at that point in the Revolution: "Before that unjust Tribunal, there was little or no order of procedure, ensuring to any accused person any reasonable hearing. There could have been no such Revolution, if all laws, forms, and ceremonies, had not first been so monstrously abused, that the suicidal vengeance of the Revolution was to scatter them all to the winds" (390). The use of contrasting scenes keeps before the reader the double nature of Dickens's themes. We see France in comparison to England, humanity threatened by cruelty, death overcome by resurrection, private heroism defeated by public vengeance, human love surviving irrational hate.

At the heart of these double themes is a critique of what Thomas Carlyle had called "the Age of Machinery" in his 1829 essay "Signs of the Times," a mechanistic view of human affairs that Dickens saw as characterizing the revolutionary period as well. In modern England it was evident in the changes brought about by the Industrial Revolution; a large portion of the population was now subjected to long hours of mind-numbing, mechanical labor in noisy, dirty, and dehumanizing factories. But for Dickens and Carlyle the real fear of the mechanical age was the inhumanity of contemporary political theory.

Influenced by earlier economists such as Thomas Malthus, who had argued in his *Essay on the Principle of Population* (1803) that anyone who could not earn a living had no right to live at all, the political economists and statisticians had reduced human life to numbers by dealing with people in purely economic terms. In his justification of his portrayal of the French aristocrats, Dickens noted that he had relied on contemporary reports rather than on the later statistical findings of some historians: "No *ex post facto* enquiries and provings by figures will hold water, surely, against the tremendous testimony of men living at the time" (Nonesuch, 3:162).

In this mechanical age human relationships were replaced by what Carlyle termed the "Cash Nexus," where money exchanged hands in place of compassion or charity. In *A Tale of Two Cities* the Marquis exemplifies the cash nexus when he throws a coin to Gaspard to pay for the child he has just run over. The poor father replies with "a most unearthly cry, 'Dead!'" (131). Here Dickens juxtaposes most forcibly a mechanical view of life, where a child can be paid for, against the agony of a loving father.

This mechanistic age was endorsed by the Utilitarians, who argued that unless a thing (or a person) was useful, it had no value. Such an attitude was already a part of the puritanical view of life, which had a strong hold over many Victorians. With regard to art and literature it meant the rejection of any imaginative work: fairy tales were banned in some circles, and novels rejected as fiction and therefore valueless. Dickens's constant aim in his writings was to combat this depressingly mechanistic view. For Dickens the imagination is man's most valuable attribute; without it we lose our compassion, our sense of moral value, everything that makes us human. The aim of all his writing is summed up in his "Preliminary Word" at the beginning of *Household Words*: "No mere utilitarian spirit, no iron binding of the mind to grim realities, will give a harsh tone to our Household Words. In the bosoms of the young and old, of the well-to-do and of the poor, we would tenderly cherish that light of Fancy which is inherent in the human breast; which, according to its nurture, burns with an inspiring flame, or sinks into a sullen glare, but which (or woe betide that day!) can never be extinguished."

In everything Dickens and Carlyle wrote can be found an overriding concern with what Carlyle calls the dynamism of human life and with the mysteries of man's spiritual nature and imaginative powers. We have seen how Dickens emphasizes that "every human creature is constituted to be that profound secret and mystery to every other" (12) and how this secret inner life, from Manette's Bastille memories to Carton's better nature, can inspire a person to true heroism. Set against such dynamism in the main duality of the book is the mechanism of both the ancien régime and the revolutionaries, once their movement has taken hold. The stone château of the Marquis (like Stone Lodge, the home of the utilitarian businessman in *Hard Times*) is immune to human emotion; the château, like its occupant, is a blind mask, incapable of expression until at last the fire and wind, "driving straight from the infernal regions" (283), wipe away the stone faces. The stony Marquis represents the inhumanity of the old order, which treated people as though they were mere animals and whose own society was an empty sham of fine clothes, frizzled hair, and artificial complexions, disfigured by "the leprosy of unreality" (126).

Equally dehumanized, though, are the revolutionaries, who demonstrate utilitarianism's emphasis upon the group rather than the individual in the doctrine of "the greatest happiness of the greatest number." *A Tale of Two Cities* is very clearly about the value of the individual in the face of a cataclysmic social movement that swept people up into a terrifying ocean, submerging individual thought and action in the tide of mob violence and blind sheeplike conformity. The road mender who had sympathized with Gaspard at the beginning of the book becomes an inhuman and callous observer of the Terror, one of the nameless "citizens" or "Jacques" who will sacrifice all for an institution, the Republic. We see this turning of people into mechanical followers of a cause throughout the novel, and Dickens shows how it can happen regardless of the cause or its value. At Roger Cly's funeral, for example, the crowd has no idea who is being buried, but at the suggestion that there are spies involved, "the idea was so acceptable in the prevalent absence of any idea, that the crowd caught it up with eagerness" (187). Even more telling is when the mender of roads is taken to see the King and Queen by Madame Defarge, in order to whet his appetite against them and the aristocracy. The simple peasant is so taken up by the pomp and ceremony of the royal procession and the fawning crowd around it that he "bathed himself, so much to his temporary intoxication, that he cried Long live the King, Long live the Queen, Long live everybody and everything! as if he had never heard of ubiquitous Jacques in his time" (210). When it is over and the intoxication brought on by crowd action has passed, he suddenly realizes how he has been acting and fears the Defarges' wrath, but is relieved to find that they thought it was a pretence on his part.

It is against such mindless adherence to the group, such loss of personal thought and action to an identification with a cause, that the major actors in the novel have to pit themselves, at great cost. We see the duality in Miss Pross's confrontation with the implacable Madame Defarge, in the mechanical knitting of the revolutionary women contrasted with Lucie's golden thread, in Carton's humanity contrasted with the inhuman counting of the knitting women and the mechanical action of the guillotine itself.

At the center of the novel is this overturning of the natural human order, first by the members of the ancien régime whose "monstrous abuse" of their role as employers, landowners, fathers, and mothers resulted in the dehumanizing of the common people, and then by those people who have been turned into monsters by such inhuman treatment. The metaphors Dickens relies on to demonstrate this perversion of humanity are the anvil and furnace, both mechanical devices that suggest the inhuman crippling of the human spirit by the stone-faced aristocrats like the Marquis. The oppressed peasants are like a living sea, but their faces are "hardened in the furnaces of suffering until the touch of pity could make no mark on them" (268). Madame Defarge's customers pay for their wine with "battered small coins . . . as much defaced and beaten out of their original impress as the small coinage of humanity from whose ragged pockets they had come" (199). Even

Saint Antoine itself, taking on the character of its residents, is changed, its face distorted because "the image had been hammering into this [face] for hundreds of years, and the last finishing blows had told mightily on the expression" (271). In what could be called the thematic statement of the novel, Dickens relies again on the anvil metaphor: "Crush humanity out of shape once more, under similar hammers, and it will twist itself into the same tortured forms" (459). The contrast between the mechanical and the dynamic, between soul-destroying machine and malleable humanity, is constantly reiterated in such metaphors and is reinforced by the frighteningly graphic machines of death, the grindstone and the guillotine.

A Tale of Two Cities is perhaps Dickens's most Christian novel, and he emphasizes the perversion of Christianity that took place during the Revolution to demonstrate the "frightful moral disorder, born of unspeakable suffering, intolerable oppression, and heartless indifference" (428) that marked the Terror. Christianity was outlawed, its buildings closed, and its practices forbidden during the Revolution (Dickens's friend Wilkie Collins wrote a story based on the practice of holding religious services secretly on boats off the French coast). The Convention even approved the worship of a Goddess of Reason, whose feast was celebrated at Notre Dame. The guillotine replaced the cross as the people's salvation: "It was the sign of the regeneration of the human race. It superseded the Cross. Models of it were worn on breasts from which the Cross was discarded, and it was bowed down to and believed in where the Cross was denied" (336). The guillotine was even canonized, and the wood-sawyer calls his saw "Little Sainte Guillotine" (342). In her role as revolutionary leader, inspiring her fellow citizens to action, Madame Defarge was "a Missionary—there were many like her—such as the world will do well never to breed again" (224). Again Dickens dramatizes the struggle between good and evil as a contrast between an imaginative, human belief and the perversion of it into a mechanical reverence for reason and worship of a blind vengeance.

Perhaps the most striking image of the contrast between vital, human love and its perverted revolutionary form occurs in Dickens's description of the carmagnole, the mad dance associated with the Revolution. What should be a celebration of humanity's sense of music, harmony, rhythmic movement, and fellowship has become a travesty of all those qualities: "They danced to the popular Revolution song, keeping a ferocious time that was like a gnashing of teeth in unison. . . . No fight could have been half so terrible as this dance. It was so emphatically a fallen sport—a something, once innocent, delivered over to all devilry—a healthy pastime changed into a means of angering the blood, bewildering the senses, and steeling the heart. Such grace as was visible in it, made it the uglier, showing how warped and perverted all things good by nature were become" (342–43). Dickens juxtaposes natural, human love with this frightening perversion of love into lust and sensuality when, as the carmagnole dancers sweep past Charles and Lucie, he "held her to his heart and turned her beautiful head between his face and the brawling crowd, so that his tears and her lips might come together unseen" (353). This picture of pure human love sheltering itself from the abased violence of the carmagnole is repeated by Carton and the little seamstress, the counterparts of Darnay and Lucie, when they ride in the tumbril together: "He gently places her with her back to the crashing engine that constantly whirrs up and falls, and she looks into his face and thanks him. . . . Eye to eye, voice to voice, hand to hand, heart to heart, these two children of the Universal Mother, else so wide apart and differing, have come together on the dark highway, to repair home together, and to rest in her bosom" (462–63).

In these two images of a man and a woman united in love against the violence and degradation of the Terror Dickens expresses his main hope for the human race. By using dualities to work out his "tale" and its themes, he counters mob destruction with personal heroism, public irresponsibility with private integrity. Even though he asks, "What private solicitude could rear itself against the deluge of the Year One of Liberty" (335), the private life as demonstrated by Lucie's golden thread and Carton's secretive sacrifice is seen to exemplify what is best in human affairs. While the mob is fickle and changeable, Lucie in particular demonstrates loyalty and faithfulness to the death. While the mob acts irrationally, driven ostensibly by a cause but acting often out of blind fury, the honest individual acts out of a sense of duty and honor. Such a sense draws Darnay back to Paris, shamed into a sense of his own duties to his tenants by the knowledge that his servant Gabelle is threatened with the guillotine because of his fidelity to his master Darnay. Duty sustains Lucie when Darnay is in prison, just as it gives Miss Pross the strength to overcome Madame Defarge. It is a sense of duty to Lucie that gives Carton his new interest in life and allows him to overcome his inertia and take over the initiative when Doctor Manette fails.

From its opening statement, "It was the best of times; it was the worst of times," A Tale of Two Cities moves the reader through a world of paradox and contradiction, of people being "buried alive," of a dissolute, wasted man performing a sublime action, until at the end the great Christian paradox of the Resurrection is realized with Sydney Carton's victory of love over Madame Defarge's implacable hate. In the working out of these paradoxes A Tale of Two Cities looks back to the attitudes of the romantic writers who were so influenced by the French Revolution. Like the generation of writers who preceded him, Dickens sees the need for revolution but recognizes the dangers of mass action. Like the romantics, he sees a new world and a new vision coming about through the spiritual revolution of the individual. Carton's prophetic vision of "a beautiful city and a brilliant people rising from this abyss" (465) echoes the prophetic writing of Blake, Coleridge, and Wordsworth, who also saw the fallen world being re-born, not through revolution, but through the individual imagination and the individual's capacity for love.

appendix:

How A *Tale of Two Cities* Was Serialized

A Tale of Two Cities was published simultaneously in weekly parts in *All the Year Round* and in monthly parts throughout 1859. The following list shows how the chapters were divided by the two methods of publication.

ALL THE YEAR ROUND

30 April	Book 1	Chapters 1–3
7 May		Chapter 4
14 May		Chapter 5
21 May		Chapter 6
28 May	Book 2	Chapters 1–2
4 June		Chapter 3
11 June		Chapters 4–5
18 June		Chapter 6
25 June		Chapters 7–8
2 July		Chapter 9
9 July		Chapters 10–11
16 July		Chapters 12–13
23 July		Chapter 14
30 July		Chapter 15
6 August		Chapter 16
13 August		Chapters 17–18
20 August		Chapters 19–20

27 August		Chapter 21
3 September		Chapters 22–23
10 September		Chapter 24
17 September	Book 3	Chapter 1
24 September		Chapters 2–3
1 October		Chapters 4–5
8 October		Chapters 6–7
15 October		Chapter 8
22 October		Chapter 9
29 October		Chapter 10
5 November		Chapters 11–12
12 November		Chapter 13
19 November		Chapter 14
26 November		Chapter 15

Monthly Parts

June	Book 1	Chapters 1–6
July	Book 2	Chapters 1–6
August	Book 2	Chapters 7–13
September	Book 2	Chapters 14–18
October	Book 2	Chapters 19–24
November	Book 3	Chapters 1–7
December	Book 3	Chapters 8–15

notes and references

1. Dickens's Times

1. *A Tale of Two Cities*, World's Classics edition (Oxford: Oxford University Press, 1988), 1; hereafter cited in the text by page number.

2. William Hazlitt, "Mr. Coleridge," in *The Spirit of the Age* (1825; Oxford: Oxford University Press, 1966), 47.

3. *The Letters of Charles Dickens*, 3 vols., Nonesuch edition, ed. Walter Dexter (Bloomsbury: Nonesuch Press, 1938), 2:651–52; hereafter cited in the text as Nonesuch.

2. The Importance of the Work

1. *Christmas Books*, World's Classics edition (Oxford: Oxford University Press, 1988), 9; hereafter cited in the text as *CB*.

3. Critical Reception

1. *Eclectic Review*, October 1861, 458; hereafter cited in the text as *Eclectic*.

2. *Athenaeum*, 10 December 1859, 774.

3. *Saturday Review*, 17 December 1859, 741–43. Reprinted in *The Dickens Critics*, ed. George H. Ford and Lauriat Lane, Jr. (Ithaca, N.Y.: Cornell University Press, 1961), 40–41; hereafter cited in the text as Stephen.

4. *Dublin University Magazine*, 55 (February 1860): 239.

5. See *Critic* n.s. 19(17 December 1859): 602–3.

6. Letter to John Forster, 26 October 1859, in *New Letters of Thomas Carlyle*, ed. Alexander Carlyle (London and New York: Bodley Head, 1904), 205.

7. *Examiner,* 10 December 1859, 788–89.

8. John Forster, *The Life of Charles Dickens,* ed. A. J. Hoppé (London: J. M. Dent, 1966), 2:282; hereafter cited in the text as Forster.

9. [Margaret Oliphant], "Charles Dickens," *Blackwood's Edinburgh Magazine* 109(June 1871): 691.

10. George Gissing, *Charles Dickens: A Critical Study* (London: Blackie, 1898), 61; hereafter cited in the text as Gissing.

11. Sir George Saintsbury, *Essays in English Literature* (London: J. M. Dent, 1895), 370.

12. A. W. Ward, *Dickens* (London: Macmillan, 1882), 157; hereafter cited in the text as Ward.

13. See Edgar Shannon, "The Dramatic Element in Dickens," *Sewanee Review* 21(1913): 277–86.

14. Edwin Percy Whipple, *Charles Dickens: The Man and His Work,* 2 vols. (Boston and New York: Houghton Mifflin, 1912), 200; hereafter cited in the text as Whipple.

15. Arthur Waugh, "Introducing *A Tale of Two Cities,*" *Dickensian* 23(1926–27): 15.

16. Bernard Darwin, *Dickens* (London: Duckworth, 1933), 117–18.

17. G. K. Chesterton, *Charles Dickens* (London: Methuen, 1906), 230–31.

18. George Orwell, "Charles Dickens," in *Decline of the English Murder and Other Essays* (1939; London: Penguin, 1965), 92.

19. George H. Ford, *Dickens and His Readers: Aspects of Novel-Criticism since 1836* (Princeton: Princeton University Press, 1955), 37.

20. Angus Wilson, *The World of Charles Dickens* (London: Martin Secker & Warburg, 1970), 261.

21. Heinz Reinhold, "Charles Dickens' Roman 'A Tale of Two Cities' und das Publikum," *Germanische-romanische-Monatsschrift* 36 (1955): 319–37.

22. Fred Kaplan, *Dickens: A Biography* (New York: William Morrow, 1988), 417.

23. Lawrence Frank, "Dickens' *A Tale of Two Cities*: The Poetics of Impasse," *American Imago* 36 (1979): 218.

24. Albert D. Hutter, "Nation and Generation in *A Tale of Two Cities,*" *PMLA* 93(1978): 455–56.

25. T. A. Jackson, *Charles Dickens: The Progress of a Radical* (New York: International Publishers, 1938), 173.

26. Georg Lukács, *The Historical Novel,* trans. Hannah and Stanley Mitchell (London, 1962), 243; as quoted in Andrew Sanders, *The Victorian Historical Novel 1840–1880* (London: Macmillan, 1978), 74.

27. Morton Dauwen Zabel, "The Revolutionary Fate: *A Tale of Two Cities*," in *Craft and Character in Modern Fiction* (New York: Viking Press, 1957), 69.

28. Avrom Fleishman, "Dickens: Visions of Revolution," in *The English Historical Novel* (Baltimore and London: Johns Hopkins University Press, 1971), 123.

29. Andrew Sanders, "The Track of a Storm: Charles Dickens's Historical Novels,"in *The Victorian Historical Novel 1840–1880,* 93.

30. Sylvère Monod, "*A Tale of Two Cities*: A French View," *Dickens Memorial Lectures, 1970, Dickensian* 65, suppl. (September 1970): 26–27; hereafter cited in the text as Monod.

31. John Gross, "A Tale of Two Cities," in *Dickens and the Twentieth Century,* ed. John Gross and Gabriel Pearson (London: Routledge & Kegan Paul, 1962), 194.

4. The Genesis of A Tale of Two Cities

1. See items 21 and 22 for 1855 in *Charles Dickens' Book of Memoranda,* ed. Fred Kaplan (New York: New York Public Library, 1981); hereafter cited in the text as *Memoranda.*

2. *The Letters of Charles Dickens,* ed. Burgis, House, Storey, Tillotson, Fielding, 6 vols., Pilgrim edition (Oxford: Clarendon Press, 1981), 5:383; hereafter cited in the text as *Letters.*

3. *The Heart of Charles Dickens,* ed. Edgar Johnson (New York: Duell, Sloan and Pearce, 1952), 354–55.

4. For a discussion of Dickens's debt to *The Dead Heart* see Carl R. Dolmetsch, "Dickens and *The Dead Heart,*" *Dickensian* 55(1959): 179–87.

5. The Setting: Revolutionary France

1. Charles Dickens the younger in his Introduction to the Macmillan edition of *A Tale of Two Cities* (1902); quoted by Andrew Sanders in "'Cartloads of Books': Some Sources for *A Tale of Two Cities,*" in *Dickens and Other Victorians,* ed. Joanne Shattock (London: Macmillan, 1988), 40.

2. [Percy Fitzgerald], "The Eve of the Revolution," *Household Words* 17:592.

3. Jean-Jacques Rousseau, *The Confessions of Jean Jacques Rousseau,* 2 vols., Everyman edition (London: J. M. Dent, 1943), 1:149.

4. Thomas Carlyle, *The French Revolution: A History,* World's Classics

edition (Oxford: Oxford University Press, 1989), 1:200; hereafter cited in the text as *FR*.

5. Hedva Ben-Israel, *English Historians on the French Revolution* (Cambridge: Cambridge University Press, 1968), 111.

7. The Plot

1. *David Copperfield*, World's Classics edition (Oxford: Oxford University Press, 1983), 706.

2. *Great Expectations* (London: Penguin, 1965), 330.

10. "Buried Alive"

1. Philip Collins, *Dickens and Crime* (London: Macmillan, 1962), 117. Collins provides an excellent survey of the influence of Dickens's prison visits on *A Tale of Two Cities*.

2. *American Notes and Pictures from Italy*, New Oxford Illustrated edition (Oxford: Oxford University Press, 1966), 99.

3. Stanley Tick has argued this point forcibly in "Cruncher on Resurrection: A Tale of Charles Dickens," *Renascence* 33(1981): 86–98.

11. Women and Marriage

1. According to Dickens's friend Edmund Yates, Stryver was based on a real lawyer, Edwin James, "a fat, florid man, with a large bland face . . . his practice was extensive, his fees enormous." Yates took Dickens to see James in 1858 or 1859 and, commenting on the resemblance when he read the first Stryver number, claims that Dickens replied, "Not bad I think, especially after only one sitting." After being disbarred in England, James practiced in the United States. See p. 487.

12. Patterns of Imagery

1. Harland S. Nelson traces some similarities in Dickens's use of the shadow motif and the use of the motif in a romance called *The Substance and the Shadow*, which was serialized in a London weekly paper in 1859. See "Shadow and Substance in *A Tale of Two Cities*," *Dickensian* 84(1988):97–106.

13. "A Tale of Two Cities"

1. For a detailed study of the links between the three fountains in the novel see Ewald Mengel, "The Poisoned Fountain: Dickens's Use of a Traditional Symbol in *A Tale of Two Cities*," *Dickensian* 80(1984):26–32.

selected bibliography

Primary Works

A Tale of Two Cities was first published in weekly installments in *All the Year Round* from 30 April to 26 November 1859. It appeared simultaneously in monthly parts from June to December of that year and was published in book form in November 1859 with illustrations by Hablot Knight Browne, Dickens's longtime friend and illustrator. For a listing of the weekly and monthly parts see the appendix.

Charles Dickens' Book of Memoranda. A Photographic and Typographic Facsimile of the Notebook Begun in 1855. Edited by Fred Kaplan. New York: New York Public Library, 1981. From the Original Manuscript in the Berg Collection, New York Public Library, New York.

The Letters of Charles Dickens. Edited by Walter Dexter. 3 vols. Bloomsbury: Nonesuch Press, 1938.

The Letters of Charles Dickens. Edited by Madeline House, Graham Storey, Kathleen Tillotson, Kenneth Fielding, and Nina Burgis. Pilgrim edition. 6 vols. to date (for the years to 1852). Oxford: Clarendon Press, 1965–.

Secondary Works

Reviews of *A Tale of Two Cities*

Christopher Grim [pseud.]. "My Club Table." *Dublin University Magazine* 55 (February 1860): 238–39.

Selected Bibliography

[John Forster.] "*A Tale of Two Cities.*" *Examiner,* 10 December 1859, 788–89. Reprinted in *Dickens: The Critical Heritage,* 424–26. Edited by Philip Collins. London: Routledge & Kegan Paul, 1971.

"Mr. Dickens and the Philosophy of History." *Critic* n.s. 19 (17 December 1859): 602–3.

"Our Library Table." *Athenaeum,* 10 December 1859, 774.

[Sir James Fitzjames Stephen.] "*A Tale of Two Cities.*" *Saturday Review,* 17 December 1859, 741–43. Reprinted in *The Dickens Critics.* Edited by George H. Ford and Lauriat Lane, Jr., 38–46. Ithaca, N.Y.: Cornell University Press, 1961.

Criticism of A Tale of Two Cities

Alter, Robert. "The Demons of History in Dickens' *Tale.*" *Novel* 2(1969): 135–42. Good discussion of darkness and light, religious aspects.

Arnold, Beth R. "Disraeli and Dickens on Young England." *Dickensian* 63(1967): 26–31. The influence of Disraeli's novel *Sybil* on *A Tale of Two Cities.*

Beckwith, Charles E., ed. *Twentieth Century Interpretations of "A Tale of Two Cities."* Englewood Cliffs, N.J.: Prentice-Hall, 1972. Useful collection of excerpts from major studies of the novel.

Collins, Philip. "A Tale of Two Novels: *A Tale of Two Cities* and *Great Expectations* in Dickens' Career." *Dickens Studies Annual* 2(1972): 336–51. Informative overview of the novel and its reception.

Dickens Studies Annual 12(1983). Contains 11 studies of the novel on a variety of topics.

Dolmetsch, Carl R. "Dickens and *The Dead Heart.*" *Dickensian* 55(1959): 179–87. Traces the possible influence of this obscure play on the novel.

Elliott, Ralph W. V. *A Critical Commentary on Dickens's "A Tale of Two Cities."* London: Macmillan, 1966. Excellent short study.

Fielding, K. J. "Separation—and 'A Tale of Two Cities.'" In *Charles Dickens: A Critical Introduction.* 154–68. London: Longmans, Green, 1958. Useful biographical reading.

Fleishman, Avrom. "Dickens: Visions of Revolution." In *The English Historical Novel.* 102–26. Baltimore and London: Johns Hopkins University Press, 1971. Useful historical approach that concentrates on the rebirth motif.

Frank, Lawrence. "Dickens' *A Tale of Two Cities*: The Poetics of Impasse." *American Imago* 36(1979):215–44. Applied psychoanalysis.

Friedman, Barton R. "Antihistory: Dickens' *A Tale of Two Cities.*" In *Fabri-*

cating History: English Writers on the French Revolution. 145–71. Princeton: Princeton University Press, 1988. Interesting discussion of the religious and gothic elements.

Gold, Joseph. "'The Resurrection and the Life': *A Tale of Two Cities.*" In *Charles Dickens: Radical Moralist.* 231–40. Minneapolis: University of Minnesota Press, 1972. Religious interpretation of the two cities as Babylon and Jerusalem. Well argued.

Goldberg, Michael. "Revolution: *A Tale of Two Cities.*" In *Carlyle and Dickens.* 100–128. Athens: University of Georgia Press, 1972. Very comprehensive discussion of the influence of Carlyle.

Gross, John. "A Tale of Two Cities." In *Dickens and the Twentieth Century.* Edited by John Gross and Gabriel Pearson, 187–97. London: Routledge & Kegan Paul, 1962. Well-known but rather trivial essay.

Hutter, Albert D. "Nation and Generation in *A Tale of Two Cities.*" *PMLA* 93(1978): 448–62. Complex and important reading.

———."The Novelist as Resurrectionist: Dickens and the Dilemma of Death." *Dickens Studies Annual* 12(1983): 1–39. Discusses Victorian attitudes to death and burial, resurrection men.

Jackson, T. A. "The *Tale of Two Cities.*" In *Charles Dickens: The Progress of a Radical.* 170–88. New York: International Publishers, 1938. Marxist biographical reading.

McWilliams, John P., Jr. "Progress without Politics: *A Tale of Two Cities.*" *Clio* 7(1977): 19–31. Emphasizes the novel's meaning for Victorian England.

Manheim, Leonard. "A Tale of Two Characters: A Study in Multiple Projection." *Dickens Studies Annual* 1 (1970): 225–37. Biographical, psychoanalytic approach.

Marcus, David D. "The Carlylean Vision of *A Tale of Two Cities.*" *Studies in the Novel* 8(1976):56–67.

Marshall, William H. "The Method of *A Tale of Two Cities.*" *Dickensian* 58(1962): 183–89. Useful discussion of symbols and images.

Monod, Sylvère. "Some Stylistic Devices in *A Tale of Two Cities.*" In *Dickens the Craftsman: Strategies of Presentation.* Edited by Robert B. Partlow Jr., 165–86. Carbondale: Southern Illinois University Press, 1970. Discusses repetition, cumulative effects, imagery, revolutionary style.

———. "*A Tale of Two Cities*: A French View." In *Dickens Memorial Lectures, 1970. Dickensian* 65, suppl. (September 1970): 21–37. Lively discussion.

———. "Two Interludes: Social and Historical Novels." In *Dickens the Novelist.* 440–43; 452–71. Norman: University of Oklahoma Press, 1968. Expanded translation of his *Dickens Romancier* (Paris: Hachette, 1953).

Selected Bibliography

Entertaining if critical assessment, tempered in the preceding *Dickensian* article.

Oddie, William. "*A Tale of Two Cities*." In *Dickens and Carlyle: The Question of Influence*. 61–85. London: Centenary Press, 1972. Very comprehensive study of Carlyle's influence.

Rance, Nicholas. "Charles Dickens: *A Tale of Two Cities* (1859)." In *The Historical Novel and Popular Politics in Nineteenth-Century England*. 83–101. London: Vision Press, 1975. Useful discussion of Victorian attitudes to the Revolution.

Sanders, Andrew. "'Cartloads of Books': Some Sources for *A Tale of Two Cities*." In *Dickens and Other Victorians*. Edited by Joanne Shattock, 37–52. London: Macmillan, 1988. Useful recent survey of influences on the novel.

————. "The Track of a Storm: Charles Dickens's Historical Novels." In *The Victorian Historical Novel 1840–1880*. 68–96. London: Macmillan, 1978. Worthwhile historical reading.

Slater, Michael. "The Bastille Prisoner: A Reading Dickens Never Gave." *Etudes Anglaises* 23(1970): 190–96.

Stange, G. Robert. "Dickens and the Fiery Past: *A Tale of Two Cities* Reconsidered." *English Journal* 46(1957): 381–90. Excellent discussion of themes, images.

Sterrenburg, Lee. "Psychoanalysis and the Iconography of Revolution." *Victorian Studies* 19(1975): 241–64. Interesting discussion of revolution and cannibalism.

Stoehr, Taylor. *Dickens: the Dreamer's Stance*. 1–33; 195–203. Ithaca, N.Y.: Cornell University Press, 1965. Excellent detailed discussion of style, metaphor.

Tick, Stanley. "Cruncher on Resurrection: A Tale of Charles Dickens." *Renascence* 33(1981): 86–98. Biographical approach focusing on Cruncher.

Wagenknecht, Edward. "A Tale of Two Cities." In *Dickens and the Scandalmongers*. 121–31. Norman: University of Oklahoma Press, 1965. Excellent short article.

Zabel, Morton Dauwen. "The Revolutionary Fate: *A Tale of Two Cities*." In *Craft and Character in Modern Fiction*. 49–69. New York: Viking Press, 1957. Useful and wide-ranging discussion of critical reception, historical importance, and Carton's role.

Biographies of Dickens

Forster, John. *The Life of Charles Dickens*. 3 vols. London: Chapman and Hall, 1872–74. Reprinted, edited by A. J. Hoppé, London: J. M. Dent, 1966.

Johnson, Edgar. *Charles Dickens: His Tragedy and Triumph*. 2 vols. Boston: Little, Brown; London: Hamish Hamilton, 1952.

Kaplan, Fred. *Dickens: A Biography*. New York: William Morrow, 1988.

Bibliographies

Dickens Studies Newsletter (now *Dickens Quarterly*). Contains a comprehensive listing of the latest criticism of Dickens, as well as current film and stage adaptations.

Ford, George H., ed. *Victorian Fiction: A Second Guide to Research*. New York: Modern Language Association, 1978. A short outline of useful studies of the novel appears on pp. 103–4.

Gold, Joseph. *The Stature of Dickens: A Centenary Bibliography*. Toronto: University of Toronto Press, 1971, 163–67. Material on the novel from 1859 to 1969 is listed on pp. 163–67, including several editions with introductions.

Garland Publishing's annotated bibliography of *A Tale of Two Cities* will be published in 1991.

index

Because this book is about one novel, an index to themes and characters would not be helpful as such references occur on almost every page. The index is therefore limited to references to Dicken's works other than *A Tale of Two Cities*, and to other literary works, writers, and people mentioned in the text.

the author

Ruth Glancy, lecturer of English at the University of Alberta and Concordia College in Edmonton, Canada, received her Ph.D from the University of London with a dissertation on Dickens and the short story. After teaching in Bristol for several years she returned to Canada in 1980. She is the author of several articles and reviews on Dickens and has edited Dickens's *Christmas Books* for Oxford University Press's World's Classics series. Her *Dickens's Christmas Books, Christmas Stories and Other Short Fiction: An Annotated Bibliography* appeared in 1985, and she is working on the *Tale of Two Cities* volume for the same series.